Saving the

Children

Serious Christian Parenting

by
Jack Michael

Saving the Children

ISBN 0-9717827-0-9
Copyright © 2002 by Jack Michael

Saving the Children

Published by
Jack Michael Outreach Ministries
P. O. Box 10688
Winston-Salem, NC 27108-0688

Facsimile (336) 771-9698

AUTHOR'S NOTE: Throughout this book, there are words or phrases enclosed in parentheses within a quoted portion of scripture. Although these words and phrases are not an actual part of the scripture, they are, in fact, explanations or emphases derived from scriptural word studies.

Saving the Children

This book is dedicated to my wife, Barbara, who diligently and consistently brought up our children in the nurture and admonition of the Lord, training them up in the way they should go.

Table of Contents

Introduction

Many good Christian books have been written about the plight of today's children and young people...

- ✓ Books about the dangers of alcohol and drug abuse.
- ✓ Books about blasphemous Rock and Roll music.
- ✓ Books about the pitfalls of pre-marital sex.
- ✓ Books about the proliferation of child pornography and child abuse.
- ✓ Books about the devastating problem of violence in our schools.
- ✓ Books lamenting the breakdown of the family unit in our society.
- ✓ Books warning about subtle promotion of the occult through children's books and movies about wizards and witches.

I commend every writer who has been led by the Holy Spirit to write such books, and I encourage you to purchase and read every book that will assist you in the challenging role of Christian parenting.

In this book, the Lord has directed me to write about issues somewhat different from those previously mentioned.

However, you can be assured that each subject is a valid word from the Lord to this generation of Christian parents.

And, if Jesus Christ does not return in the immediate future, the teachings will continue to apply to future generations of Christian parents, and their offspring, as we proceed further into these End Times.

Interestingly, every generation of Christian parents seem to think their generation is the last generation.

Christian parents frequently believe their children will not have to go through what they went through, because Jesus Christ will soon return, and we will all be raptured.

Yet, what I am hearing from the Lord is: **PREPARE THE NEXT GENERATION.** One specific scripture the Holy Spirit continues to impress upon my heart is Psalm 71:18:

"Now also when I am old and grayheaded, O God, do not forsake me, until I declare Your strength to this generation, your power to everyone who is to come."

8

In this book, some will likely think I was too harsh in the way I presented the truth of God's Word. In defense, I would say that too many Christian parents are trying to loosely hold on to the truth of God's Word, while at the same time, bring up their children in an atmosphere of tolerance.

The results are almost always predictable. Tolerance erodes truth, and in the process of time, tolerance will replace truth.

This is not the time for compromising the truth of God's Word. These are the days for SERIOUS CHRISTIAN PARENTING.

For a number of years, the Holy Spirit has been impressing upon me, that one strong work the Lord is doing in these End Times is RESTORING THE FEAR OF THE LORD.

I am talking about showing respect for the Lord, and respect for his Word. I am talking about honoring God, being reverent toward him, and being in awe of him.

In this book, I have attempted to convey this emphasis. Psalm 19:9 reminds us:

"The fear of the LORD is clean (or pure), *enduring forever; the judgments of the LORD are true and righteous altogether."*

Please notice from the previous scripture, the fear of the Lord ENDURES FOREVER. It will endure this generation; it will endure the next generation, and it will endure every succeeding generation.

It is time for Christian parents to once again emphasize the fear of the Lord in the arena of child rearing. These are the days of SERIOUS CHRISTIAN PARENTING.

"...whoever causes one of these little ones who believe in Me to sin, it would be better for him if a millstone were hung around his neck, and he were drowned in the depth of the sea."

Jesus Christ
Matthew 18:6

Book One

The Battle for the Souls of the Children

Chapter One

Upon your Sons and Daughters

"And it shall come to pass in the last days, says God, that I will pour out of My Spirit on all flesh; your sons and your daughters shall prophesy, your young men shall see visions, your old men shall dream dreams, and on My menservants and on my maidservants I will pour out My Spirit in those days; and they shall prophesy." (Acts 2:17-18).

Several times, I have had the privilege of traveling to the Solomon Islands as part of a Gospel crusade team. For those who are unfamiliar with the Solomon Islands, they are a large group of islands, which lie north of Australia, and east of Papua New Guinea.

We were very impressed with the young people in the Solomon Islands. Never before had I seen young people with so much zeal for the Lord.

During our evening crusade meetings and morning seminars, the young people always arrived first, and quickly filled up the front rows.

During times of praise and worship, these young people would sing with all their might, clap their hands, and dance before the Lord. They would unashamedly lift their hands to the Lord, tears streaming down their faces, and worship God with all their heart.

I am talking specifically about teenagers, and even children. Never before had I seen anything comparable, whether in America, or any other nation where I have ministered.

We asked those who invited us, *"What is happening with your young people?"* They replied, *"We don't know. It's just a sovereign move of God."* We said, *"Tell us more."*

They began to share how groups of these young people would go up to the mountains and pray all night. The next morning they would come down into the open-air market and preach the gospel of Jesus Christ, and adults were getting saved!

Sometimes, groups of these young people would go into the mountains for three days to fast and pray for their nation.

I thought about the young people in our American churches. They might go to the mountains for a white water rafting trip with the youth group, but I don't know about fasting and praying?

During our times in the Solomon Islands, teenagers would look us in the eye, and say, *"We are going to take our nation for God, and then we're going to the other nations!"*

During my second trip to the Solomon Islands, I had a dream. In the dream, I saw American young people roaming through a neighborhood, shooting and killing adults.

They did not seem to be organized, nor did they seem to have a cause. A young man was doing the shooting, and he was just indiscriminately firing at adults, and seemed to be having fun doing so!

I did not immediately tell anyone about the dream. I began to pray, and I was more than willing for God to say, *"It was just a dream. It has no significance."*

Instead, after two weeks of prayer, the Spirit of the Lord spoke to me:

What you saw in the dream does not have to happen, but in order for the youth of America to be turned, there must be revival in the schools.

Now, I was prepared to hear the Holy Spirit say there must be revival in the church youth groups.

I was also prepared to hear God say there must be restoration in the family, and revival in our homes.

But, I was greatly surprised to hear the Holy Spirit say: THERE MUST BE REVIVAL IN THE SCHOOLS.

However, when you stop to think about the situation, it makes perfect sense. Most of the children and young people in America do not live in a Christian home, nor do they belong to a church youth group. How else can God reach this generation unless there is revival in the schools?

About now, some of you are probably wondering how the Lord is going to avoid clashing with the United States Supreme Court on the matter of Separation of Church and State? Well, quite frankly, God is not hindered by such things!

IF THE LORD WANTS REVIVAL IN THE SCHOOLS, THERE WILL BE REVIVAL IN THE SCHOOLS!

In the days that followed, I continued to pray about these matters, not being totally settled in my spirit. Soon, the Holy Spirit spoke to me again. He said:

If this generation of adults will not turn from their sin, and begin to embrace the standards of my Word (the Bible), I will pass over this generation of adults, and pour out my Spirit on their children.

Initially, I had a little trouble accepting this word from the Lord. Passing over an entire generation of adults just did not seem like something God would do. Rather quickly, the Spirit of the Lord reminded me, *"I have already done so before!"*

Immediately, I remembered the story from Numbers, chapters 13-14, when the children of Israel sent 12 spies to spy out the land of Canaan. Joshua and Caleb brought back a good report, but the other ten spies brought back an evil report, saying: *"...we are not able to go up against the people, for they are stronger than we."*

The children of Israel listened to the evil report, and refused to go in and possess the land promised to them by God. As a result, in Numbers 14:29-32, the Lord said:

"In this desert your bodies will fall – every one of you twenty years old or more who was counted in the census, and who has grumbled against me. Not one of you will enter the land I swore with uplifted hand to make your home, except Caleb son of Jephunneh and Joshua son of Nun. As for YOUR CHILDREN that you said would be taken as plunder, I will bring them in to enjoy the land you have rejected. But you – your bodies will fall in this desert." (NIV).

Literally, due to their disobedience, the Lord passed over an entire generation of adults!

Please do not misunderstand. When the Lord impressed upon me that he would pass over this generation of adults, I am sure he was not referring to those adults who are godly people. Obviously, godly adults from this generation, and succeeding generations, will continue to qualify for the outpouring of God's Holy Spirit.

Equally obvious is the fact that adults of this generation, and succeeding generations, can still accept Jesus Christ as their Savior. At the end of Joel's prophecy, as recorded in Acts, chapter two, the Bible says:

"And it shall come to pass that whoever calls on the name of the Lord shall be saved." (Acts 2:21).

The Lord was referring to this generation of adults who are wicked and selfish. Those who hate God, or deny his existence; those who pursue ungodliness; those whose lives reflect the words of the Prophet, Isaiah:

"Woe to those who call evil good, and good evil; Who put darkness for light, and light for darkness; Who put bitter for sweet, and sweet for bitter!" (Isaiah 5:20).

And now, for the GOOD NEWS!

There are some who question whether the youth of this generation can be saved. With all the rebellion, stubbornness, and outbursts of anger and violence demonstrated by this generation of young people, many wonder if there is any hope?

But, let's recall our opening scriptures in this chapter from Acts 2:17-18:

"And it shall come to pass in the last days, says God, that I will pour out of My Spirit on all flesh; your SONS and your DAUGHTERS shall prophesy; your young men shall see visions, your old men shall dream dreams. And on My menservants and on My maidservants I will pour out My Spirit in those days; and they shall prophesy."

The words, SONS and DAUGHTERS, can obviously mean succeeding generations, but also, they can literally refer to actual children.

I always imagined the young men seeing visions, the old men dreaming dreams, and the Holy Spirit being poured out upon the menservants and maidservants, but somehow, I overlooked the children.

In the days following my encounters with the Lord (as previously explained), I have been observing the young people here in America. And, you know what? The outpouring of God's Holy Spirit has begun. Everywhere I look, I am seeing signs of revival among our young people.

And, here is more good news. Much of my ministry has been in foreign countries, and everywhere I go, I am seeing the same thing. God's Holy Spirit is being poured out upon this generation of children and young people all over the world.

I believe we are on the verge of a great and mighty revival among the children and young people of the whole world.

When I use the phrase, *"This Generation,"* I am not limiting the move of God to a set number of years. I believe the outpouring of the Holy Spirit is a specific sign of these End Times, in which children now born, and children yet to be born will experience a fresh, new outpouring of God's Spirit.

The Lord is not going to be outdone by the devil. The heart of Jesus still cries out: *"...Let the little children come to me, and do not hinder them, for the kingdom of God belongs to such as these."* (Mark 10:14 NIV).

Now, listen carefully to some final words of exhortation…

All my life, having grown up in the church, I have heard ministers of the Gospel urgently plead with God's people to pray for revival.

This is good, but it seems to me that the emphasis was always on praying for revival in the church!

Will you now join me in praying for revival in the schools?

- ✓ Pray for revival on the campuses of our colleges and universities,
- ✓ Pray for revival in the high schools,
- ✓ Pray for revival in the middle schools,
- ✓ Pray for revival even at the elementary school level.

And, what about the churches?

In the coming days, churches that make a place for the outpouring of God's Holy Spirit upon the children and young people, will be churches that are *"bursting at the seams"* with growth and fruitfulness.

Unfortunately, those churches that do not recognize, or refuse to receive this move of God, will become dried up churches, full of old people.

Chapter Two

Children at War

Just as we were preparing to return to the Solomon Islands for a third crusade, civil war broke out in that island nation.

I don't know all the political ramifications, but reportedly, due to long standing hatred and jealousies, inhabitants from the island of Guadalcanal rose up against those from the island of Malaita.

It was almost like returning to pre-World War II days, when a tribal society of headhunters and cannibals paddled their canoes from island to island, to engage in warfare with one another.

The civil war primarily took place on the main island of Guadalcanal; a very familiar name to those with a historical knowledge of World War II. As you can probably imagine, this was also where our crusade was to have been conducted.

Of course, the crusade was postponed, and we were greatly disappointed. However, our greatest concern was the possibility that the ravages of civil war would quench the move of God's Spirit.

Although we wrote letters, sent facsimiles, and attempted to make phone calls in order to assess the situation in the Solomons, we received no word whatsoever.

On rare occasions, I would hear very brief reports from various world news agencies. The Solomon Islands is not a big player on the world stage.

These reports always focused on things such as: collapse of the economy, loss of tourist dollars, or New Zealand sending ships to evacuate its citizens. What I desired to hear about was the young people!

Finally, after two full years, a member of the evangelical association that invited us to the Solomon Islands sent a facsimile, and reported, *"Our nation is devastated. Many of our young men are slain!"*

Subsequently, I received a letter from a pastor in the Solomon Islands, who reported, *"A lot of young people got involved in the ethnic violence, thinking they were defending the rights of their particular group."*

Satan distorts justice. He creates ungodly causes, which appear to be just to those who have no spiritual discernment. Then, he stirs up those causes, like throwing fuel on fire!

This pastor added a further observation: *"The church,"* he emphasized, *"should have raised its standard of righteousness before the ethnic tension erupted!"*

Because of my concern about the young people, I prayed often about the situation in the Solomon Islands.

You see, this civil war did not occur only because of political unrest or ethnic tensions. Yes, Satan is the instigator of all such unrest, but during these End Times, he has a much larger agenda in mind than just politics.

All over the world, Satan and his agents are stirring up civil unrest within nations, and causing strife between nations. Then, when the unrest erupts into warfare, he is causing THE CHILDREN to be pushed to the forefront of the battle.

Just think about it. Over the past several decades, how many reports of civil wars and revolutions have you heard about? And, how often do those reports include accounts of children being armed by guerilla forces, and put into the forefront of battle?

Undoubtedly, everyone in the world who owns a television set has repeatedly seen film footage of Palestinian children throwing rocks at Israeli soldiers!

Reliable sources report that throughout the Muslim world, there are thousands upon thousands of fundamentalist Islamic schools, aggressively training millions of young boys for JIHAD (Islamic Holy War). A holy war that someday will be waged against Israel, and perhaps the United States as well.

As I was writing this book, the Spirit of the Lord prompted me to alert you...

In the coming days, watch, for the time will come when we will see children as terrorists.

There is a great spiritual conflict going on here. Satan and his evil agents are thrusting children into warfare and violence in an effort to STOP THE OUTPOURING of the Holy Spirit upon the children and young people.

But, God will not be outdone by the devil. God will have a remnant, even in the Muslim countries. The outpouring of the Holy Spirit will not be stopped, not even by Islam in its most radical, militant, fundamental form.

Revelation 5:9 promises that there will be people in Heaven, *"...out of every tribe, and tongue and people and nation...."*

I have had the privilege of ministering in a Palestinian Christian church in Bethlehem, and during the altar call, laying my hands on Palestinian children and young people, and praying for God to pour out his Holy Spirit upon them.

Some of you are likely thinking, *"Thank God I live in America, and my children are not confronted with things like civil war, or preparing for Jihad."*

Yes, that is true, for the moment, but this has not deterred Satan. He has thrust young people and children to the forefront of war by bringing violence into our schools, shopping malls, and indeed, into our homes.

Even as it was in the days of Noah, so it is quickly becoming in our society. In Genesis 6:11, the Bible reported:

"The earth also was corrupt before God, and the earth was filled with violence."

So, the question before us is, how can we protect our children from the ever-increasing violence that is coming upon the earth in these last days?

Some years ago, I remember reading the account of a certain British Regiment during World War I. For four long years of front line warfare, the regiment did not have a single casualty; they did not lose even one soldier killed in action.

They could give only one explanation for this incredible miracle. Every soldier in the regiment, officers and enlisted, had been issued a copy of the 91st Psalm, and they were required to recite this psalm everyday.

By contrast, during my time in the Marine Corps, at one of my duty stations, a certain Gunnery Sergeant worked for me.

During the Vietnam War, this marine was stationed at a Fire Base in the northern part of what was at that time, South Vietnam. He shared the sad account of his time on that Fire Base. For a long period of time, more than a month, at least one marine from his battalion was killed every single day.

Quite frankly, the Word of God is the only TRULY EFFECTIVE SHIELD between God's children and the destruction that is coming upon this earth.

Through the efforts of man, security can be increased, metal detectors can be placed in the schools, and law enforcement officers can attend endless workshops and seminars. But, the truth is, the diligence of man is no match for the cleverness of the devil!

Satan will continue to devise schemes by which our children will be subject to violence. As we progress further into these End Times, the violence will not stop; it will increase.

I wish I could paint a prettier picture, and tell you the world will once again become a safe place for our children. But, the truth of the matter is this:

"...evil men and impostors will grow worse and worse, deceiving and being deceived." (2 Timothy 3:13).

Yet, there is hope. Listen to the scriptures that immediately follow the above verse:

"But you must continue in the things which you have learned and been assured of, knowing from whom you have learned them, and that from childhood you have known the Holy Scriptures, which are able to make you wise for salvation through faith which is in Christ Jesus." (2 Timothy 3:14-15).

Did you notice the influence of parenting in the previous verses? Earlier in 2 Timothy 1:5, Paul had acknowledged that influence in Timothy's life:

"When I call to remembrance the genuine faith that is in you, which dwelt first in your grandmother Lois and your mother Eunice, and I am persuaded is in you also."

These are not the days for abdicating the responsibility of parenting. These are the days for rediscovering both the responsibility and influence of parenting.

I repeat; only the authority of God's Word is a truly effective shield between us and the destruction that is coming upon this earth.

I believe this would be a good place to insert the entire 91st Psalm:

"He who dwells in the secret place of the Most High shall abide under the shadow of the Almighty. I will say of the LORD, He is my refuge and my fortress; my God, in Him I will trust. Surely He shall deliver you from the snare of the fowler and from the perilous pestilence. He shall cover you with His feathers, and under His wings you shall take refuge…

...His truth shall be your shield and buckler. You shall not be afraid of the terror by night, nor of the arrow that flies by day, nor of the pestilence that walks in darkness, nor of the destruction that lays waste at noonday. A thousand may fall at your side, and ten thousand at your right hand; but it shall not come near you. Only with your eyes shall you look, and see the reward of the wicked. Because you have made the LORD, who is my refuge, even the Most High, your dwelling place, no evil shall befall you, nor shall any plague come near your dwelling; for He shall give His angels charge over you, TO KEEP YOU (or guard you) *in all your ways. In their hands they shall bear you up, lest you dash your foot against a stone. You shall tread upon the lion and the cobra, the young lion and the serpent you shall trample underfoot. Because he has set his love upon Me, therefore I will deliver him; I will set him on high, because he has known My name. He shall call upon Me, and I will answer him; I will be with him in trouble; I will deliver him and honor him. With long life I will satisfy him, and show him My salvation."*

The Lord did not give us the 91st Psalm to use as poetry; he gave it to us for protection.

I believe it would be a wise assignment for your children to memorize the 91st Psalm.

Perhaps the whole family could memorize the psalm. Then, during family devotions, or prayers, everyone could get involved in the exercising of their faith by reciting different portions of the psalm.

You see, the key to releasing the power in the 91st Psalm is contained in verse 2:

"I WILL SAY OF THE LORD, He is my refuge and my fortress; my God, in Him I will trust."

I will **SAY** of the Lord! It is the speaking forth of God's Word that releases the power. Teach your children to open their mouths, and by faith, boldly confess, declare, and proclaim the truth of God's Word.

And, don't just do it once. This is not a little spiritual exercise that you have to hurry up and get it over with, so you can get on with your life.

Make these biblical principles a lifestyle. Not only will the Word of God protect your children from violence that is occurring all around them. God's Word will deliver your children from the schemes and devices the devil has planned against them!

Hopefully, in the future, there will be an opportunity to return to the Solomon Islands. When that time comes, most likely I will be saddened by the stories of young people who lost their lives in the civil war.

Perhaps, some of those who got caught up in the misguided fervor of civil war, and unnecessarily lost their lives, had previously attended our crusade meetings?

Yet, I also expect to be encouraged by the fact that many of those young people were not overcome by Satan's schemes, and in fact, are not only continuing to serve God, but are serving him with greater zeal and commitment than before.

In short, I expect to see that the revival has not just barely survived; I expect to see that the revival has gained momentum and is exceeding what we previously experienced!

The letter I received from the pastor in the Solomon Islands also said the following: *"We are beginning to re-gather our young people, to mobilize them, to press on until we see God glorified in our land."*

Satan will not win this war! The plans and purposes of God will prevail. Satan will not stop the outpouring of God's Holy Spirit upon this generation, and succeeding generations of children and young people.

In concluding this chapter, let me point out that I did not write this book to help God. God is not threatened by the devil. Romans 16:20 tells us:

"And the God of peace will crush Satan under your feet shortly...."

I wrote this book to help Christian parents, and to help all those who have responsibility for teaching children, and rearing children; hopefully, to prevent your children from being CHILDREN AT WAR.

You see, the unfortunate truth is, a great number of children and young people will be swept up in Satan's deceptive schemes, and will fall prey to his destructive devices.

I want your children to be included in the victory, rather than lost in the defeat. I want your children to experience the outpouring of God's Holy Spirit.

Chapter Three

The Homosexual Threat

"Therefore God also gave them up to uncleanness, in the lusts of their hearts, to dishonor their bodies among themselves, who exchanged the truth of God for the lie, and worshiped and served the creature (what God created) *rather than the Creator, who is blessed forever. Amen. For this reason God gave them up to vile passions.*

Scriptures continued, next page...

...For even their women EXCHANGED the natural use for what is against nature. Like-wise also the men, leaving the natural use of the woman, burned in their lust for one another, men with men committing what is shameful, and receiving in themselves the penalty of their error which was due. And even as they did not like to retain God in their knowledge, God gave them over to a debased mind, to do those things which are not fitting" (not proper). (Romans 1:24-28).

As stated in the Introduction to this book, many excellent Christian books have been written about the plight of today's children and young people. The dangers presented in those books are real, and the warnings should be heeded.

However, the subject I will address in this chapter is possibly the greatest threat your children will ever face.

The Deception

In the United States, and other developed nations (and increasingly in Third World countries), there is great political, social, and religious pressure being put upon our society.

38

I am speaking specifically of pressure to accept homosexuality as normal, and as an acceptable, alternative lifestyle.

On many of our college and university campuses (those so-called institutions of higher learning), it has become popular to be *"Gay,"* lesbian, or bi-sexual.

Certain proponents of homosexuality are adamantly insisting that God created them as homosexual; thus, in their understanding, making homosexuality God's will.

As a result, we now have homosexuals being ordained as ministers (ordained by man, not by God). These homosexual ministers are presiding over homosexual congregations, preaching homosexual tolerance from their pulpits, and performing same-sex marriages; all the while, claiming to be Christians.

The more blatant homosexuals are even suggesting that Jesus was a homosexual. They base their perverted thinking on such scriptures as John 21:20:

"...Peter, turning around, saw the disciple whom Jesus loved following, who also had LEANED ON HIS BREAST at the supper, and said, Lord, who is the one who betrays You?"

Jesus himself confirmed that he was not homosexual. In Matthew 5:17, he said:

"Do not think that I have come to abolish the Law or the Prophets; I have not come to abolish them but to fulfill them."

Jesus perfectly kept the Law of Moses during his earthly ministry. In the Law, given by God to Moses, it says in Leviticus 18:22, and again in Leviticus 20:13:

"You shall not lie with a male as with a woman. It is an abomination."
"If a man lies with a male as he lies with a woman, both of them have committed an abomination. They shall surely be put to death. Their blood shall be upon them."

We live in the dispensation of God's grace through Jesus Christ, and God's judgment is not as swift, or harsh, as the Law of Moses, but don't be deceived; homosexuality is still an abomination to God!

BIBLE DEFINITION: ABOMINATION – That which is often highly esteemed by man, but is detestable, and utterly disgusting to God (see Luke 16:15 from the NKJV or KJV).

Homosexuals are greatly deceived. God does not accept their lifestyle as normal, nor as an acceptable, alternative lifestyle. God's Word strongly declares:

"Do you not know that the unrighteous will not inherit the kingdom of God? Do not be deceived. Neither fornicators, nor idolaters, nor adulterers, nor HOMOSEXUALS, nor SODOMITES, nor thieves, nor covetous, nor drunkards, nor revilers, nor extortioners will inherit the kingdom of God." (1 Corinthians 6:9-10).

BIBLE DEFINITION: HOMOSEXUAL – Of uncertain affinity (uncertain attraction, uncertain relationship); soft. Figuratively speaking, a catamite (a young boy kept by a man for the purpose of sexual relations).
BIBLE DEFINITION: SODOMITE – One who lies with a male, as with a female. One who copulates with a member of the same sex.

The Degradation

What I am going to share next is not very encouraging, but in obedience to God, I must declare what he has shown me. Later, I will teach you how to guard your family against those things that are coming upon the earth.

THE DAYS ARE COMING, WHEN...

The deceiving spirits that influence people to embrace homosexuality will turn their attacks toward seducing THE CHILDREN of our society.

Currently, these evil spirits are primarily targeting young adults. Increasingly, they are targeting teenagers. But, the days are coming when these evil spirits will turn their attention toward the children!

While writing this book, I heard a report on Christian radio about a school board in one of our major American cities that was trying to enact policies, which will require teaching homosexuality as normal, beginning at the kindergarten level.

During the same period, I heard another alarming report that originated from a highly visible Christian ministry located here in the United States.

An elementary schoolgirl was asked by her mother what she learned at school that day. She innocently replied, *"I learned that I am a lesbian."*

When the shocked mother further queried her daughter as to why she thought she was a lesbian, the young girl responded, *"I don't like boys; I like girls."*

Of course, it is a natural fact of life, that prior to puberty, girls do not like boys, and boys do not like girls. However, in this case, a lesbian teacher, pushing her own ungodly agenda, was planting seeds of sin into this young child's mind.

In the coming days, the real battle will be for the minds of the children. Satan desires to program the minds of the children, so that when they do reach puberty, homosexuality will appear to be a completely acceptable, alternative lifestyle.

This elementary age schoolgirl concluded her explanation of that day's education by announcing that when she grew up, she was not going to marry a man; she was going to marry a woman!

About now, some of you are probably thinking, *"I sure am glad my children are in the church. I feel sorry for those defenseless children in the world, who do not have the support of a Christian family."*

Let me be a bit more definitive. Not only will these seducing, deceiving, homosexual spirits be attacking the defenseless children of the world. They will specifically target, and cleverly attack the OFFSPRING OF THE SAINTS.

At the time of the publishing of this book, I know of two Christian families, both of whom have daughters who have embraced lesbian lifestyles, and these are not so-called liberal Christians.

In one of these families, the father was in full-time ministry. The daughter grew up as what we call a PK (preacher's kid). During her high school years, she seemed to be solidly committed to God's Word.

The parents in the other family are strong, loving, caring, God-fearing, genuinely born again people, who embrace the Word of God as infallible truth. Reportedly, there were no lesbian tendencies in their daughter prior to being seduced by another lesbian.

The degradation that is coming upon this world will indeed be great! God's eternal Word forever reminds us:

"Righteousness exalts a nation, but sin is a reproach (shame, or disgrace) *to any people."* (Proverbs 14:34).

THE DAYS ARE COMING, WHEN...
The biggest challenge, and greatest peer pressure your teenage children will face in school is homosexuality.

➤ There was a time when smoking was the biggest problem, and greatest peer pressure our teenagers faced.
➤ There was a time when alcohol was the biggest problem, and greatest peer pressure our teenagers faced.
➤ There was a time when illegal drugs were the biggest problem, and greatest peer pressure our teenagers faced.
➤ There was a time when pre-marital sex was the biggest problem, and greatest peer pressure our teenagers faced.

These problems continue to plague our teenagers, and challenge Christian parents, but the days are coming, when the biggest problem, and greatest peer pressure your school children will face is homosexuality.

FIRST: There will be pressure upon our children to accept homosexuality as normal. Lessons will actually be taught in the class-rooms of our schools to persuade them that homosexuality is a normal lifestyle.

SECOND: Just like the other, previously stated problems, children will feel pressured to experiment with homosexual encounters, because the other kids are doing so!

THIRD: If children can be persuaded to experiment with homosexuality, then Satan will further pressure them, and entice them to eventually embrace the lifestyle.

The degradation that is coming upon this world will indeed be great!

THE DAYS ARE COMING, WHEN...

If you want your children to learn the truth about homosexuality, you will have to teach them at home, because they will learn the opposite at school.

Today, if you want your children to learn the truth about creation (rather than evolution), you must teach them at home, because they learn the opposite at school.

Similarly, because these deceiving spirits will be targeting the children, the educational system in the United States (and elsewhere), will be pressured to submit to the homo-sexual agenda, and teach homosexuality as an acceptable, alternative lifestyle.

Be alert for the changes in our laws. The changes will be quite subtle, and oftentimes, the homosexual agenda will be slipped in under the guise of other issues.

The degradation that is coming upon this world will indeed be great!

THE DAYS ARE COMING, WHEN...

A new breed of homosexuals will arise in the earth.

It has been accurately stated that many homosexuals were unwilling victims of child molestation, or incest, and these incidents in their past strongly contributed to their current homosexual lifestyles. Many also came from homes with absentee fathers.

Such people are often plagued with guilt and low self-esteem, and desperately need to experience God's love and forgiveness.

Thankfully, God's love and forgiveness, as well as his power to deliver from sin, are still available to all who desire to be free!

However, the days are coming, and have already begun, when a new breed of homosexuals will arise in the earth. We are talking about people who cannot blame the events of the past for their current choices.

Because of the sex-crazed emphasis of our society, many deluded people, who are recklessly pursuing multiple sexual partners, and more intense sexual gratification, will visit places they ought not to visit.

I am referring to places like *"Gay"* bars, illicit nightclubs, bathhouses, and massage parlors.

As a consequence, such people will be easily seduced by other homosexuals, and will, in turn, become seducers themselves. As a result, a new breed of sexual predators will arise in the earth.

The degradation that is coming upon this world will indeed be great!

THE DAYS ARE COMING, WHEN...

Homosexual rape will become a problem in our society.

Probably, some would have preferred that I leave this part out of the book, but I must obey God. You see, sin never improves a society; sin always results in degradation.

Already, homosexual rape is a problem in our prison system. Eventually, that problem will show up in our society.

In a certain church where I was allowed to teach these messages on homosexuality, a lady handed me the report of a 10-year old boy, who was kidnapped by two homosexual men, and subsequently raped and murdered.

The report was so brutal and horrifying, that I could not repeat it in this book. I was reminded of the days when the Lord sent two angels to rescue Lot and his family from the ancient city of Sodom.

That account, which is found in Genesis 19:1-13, is a lengthy portion of scripture, but I felt it was important to include the entire passage in this book.

"The two angels arrived at Sodom in the evening, and Lot was sitting in the gateway of the city. When he saw them, he got up to meet them and bowed down with his face to the ground. My lords, he said, please turn aside to your servant's house. You can wash your feet and spend the night and then go on your way early in the morning. No, they answered, we will spend the night in the square. But he insisted so strongly that they did go with him and entered his house. He prepared a meal for them, baking bread without yeast, and they ate. Before they had gone to bed, all the men from every part of the city of Sodom – both young and old – surrounded the house. They called to Lot, where are the men who came to you tonight? BRING THEM OUT TO US SO THAT WE CAN HAVE SEX WITH THEM. Lot went outside to meet them and shut the door behind him and said, No, my friends. Don't do this wicked thing.

Scriptures continued, next page...

...Look, I have two daughters who have never slept with a man. Let me bring them out to you, and you can do what you like with them. But don't do anything to these men, for they have come under the protection of my roof. Get out of our way, they replied. And they said, this fellow came here as an alien, and now he wants to play the judge! We'll treat you worse than them. They kept bringing pressure on Lot and moved forward to break down the door. But the men inside (the two angels) *reached out and pulled Lot back into the house and shut the door. Then they struck the men who were at the door of the house, young and old, with blindness so that they could not find the door. The two men said to Lot, Do you have anyone else here – sons-in-law, sons or daughters, or anyone else in the city who belongs to you? Get them out of here, because we are going to destroy this place. The outcry to the LORD against its people is so great that he has sent us to destroy it."* (NIV).

By the way, Lot was a terrible father. He actually offered his virgin daughters to a sex-crazed mob! Perhaps Lot had been living in Sodom a bit too long!

Someone gave me an article written by a man who, reportedly, was trying to discover the reality of the Bible. At the same time, he was trying very hard to be politically correct. In the article, he said Sodom and Gomorrah were destroyed because of unspecified sins.

Their sins were not unspecified. In Jude, verse 7, the Bible says the following:

"As Sodom and Gomorrah, and the cities around them in a similar manner to these, having given themselves over to sexual immorality and gone after strange flesh, are set forth as an example, suffering the vengeance of eternal fire."

The Greatest Deception

The greatest deception in this rising threat of homosexuality is the LOSS OF PEOPLE'S SOULS. Listen to God's strong emphasis from 1 Corinthians 6:9-10:

"...DO NOT BE DECEIVED. Neither fornicators, nor idolaters, nor adulterers, nor homosexuals, nor sodomites, nor thieves, nor covetous, nor drunkards, nor revilers, nor extortioners will inherit the kingdom of God."

51

THE REAL ISSUES ARE NOT...
1) Can homosexuals be good citizens?
2) Can they be good employees?
3) Can they be contributing members of society?
4) Should they have equal rights under the United States Constitution?

The real issue facing those who embrace homosexuality is...

THE ETERNAL DESTINATION OF THEIR SPIRIT AND SOUL.

Proverbs 14:12 reminds us:

"There is a way that seems right to a man, but its end is the way of death."

God does not change. His word does not change. He will never accept homosexuality as normal, nor will he accept homosexuality as an acceptable, alternative lifestyle.

Fortunately, God's mercy and grace are still available. Any homosexual, who is truly willing to repent, can still experience God's salvation and deliverance through the Lord Jesus Christ.

Chapter Four

Questions about Homosexuality, and Answers from the Bible

As I stated in the last chapter, the days are coming when, if you want your children to learn the truth about homosexuality, you will have to teach them at home, because they will learn the opposite at school.

Increasingly, our education system in the United States (and probably elsewhere) will be pressured to teach homosexuality as normal, and as an acceptable, alternative lifestyle.

When that time comes, here are some of the questions your children will probably ask, and answers from God's eternal word.

Question # 1 – Did God create certain people as homosexuals?

The answer is found in Romans, chapter one, verses 26-27:

"For this reason God gave them up to vile passions. For even their women exchanged the natural use for what is against nature. Likewise also the men, leaving the natural use of the woman, burned in their lust for one another, men with men committing what is shameful, and receiving in themselves the penalty of their error which was due."

Did you notice the word, EXCHANGED, in the above verses? Listen again to a portion of those scriptures: *"...For even their women EXCHANGED the natural use for what is against nature. Likewise also the men...."*

This word means: *"To change one thing for another,"* or *"TO CHANGE ONE THING INTO ANOTHER."*

Homosexuals were not created by God as *"Gay"* or lesbian. They changed one thing into another. They changed heterosexuality into homosexuality.

Also, from the same scriptures, notice the phrase, AGAINST NATURE: *"...For even their women exchanged the natural use for what is AGAINST NATURE. Likewise, also the men...."*

This word, NATURE, means, *"The regular law or order of nature."* It also simply means: *"Growth, or to produce (by germination or expansion)."*

So, what is the regular law or order of nature, as originally created by God? We find it in Genesis 1:27-28:

"So God created man in His own image; in the image of God He created him; MALE AND FEMALE HE CREATED THEM. Then God blessed them, and God said to them, BE FRUITFUL AND MULTIPLY: fill the earth and subdue it; have dominion over the fish of the sea, over the birds of the air, and over every living thing that moves on the earth."

Homosexual relationships do not have the capability to BE FRUITFUL AND MULTIPLY!

Homosexuality is against the regular law or order of nature as established by God in creation. Further proof of God's established order is found in Genesis 2:24:

"Therefore a man shall leave his father and mother and be joined to his wife, and they shall become one flesh."

By creation, God never intended for two men to become one flesh, nor did he intend for two women to become one flesh.

Conclusions...

According to the scriptures, it is clear that God never created anyone as homosexual.

Homosexuality is against nature; against the regular law or order of nature, which God established in creation.

Homosexuals have changed the regular law or order of nature. They have changed heterosexuality into homosexuality.

Also, God is not responsible for any such changes that occur after someone is created. Listen again to a portion of Romans 1:26-27: *"...For even THEIR WOMEN EXCHANGED the natural use for what is against nature. LIKEWISE ALSO THE MEN...."*

Question # 2 – What causes a person to become homosexual?

1) Listening to the wrong spirit:

"Now the Spirit EXPRESSLY (distinctly and specifically) *says that in latter times some will depart from the faith, GIVING HEED* (listening, paying attention) *TO DECEIVING SPIRITS and doctrines of demons, speaking lies in hypocrisy, having their own conscience seared with a hot iron, forbidding to marry, and commanding to abstain from foods which God created to be received with thanksgiving by those who believe and know the truth.* (1 Timothy 4:1-3).

The King James Version uses the words, *"...seducing spirits...."* By using both words, SEDUCING and DECEIVING, I think we get an accurate description of the evil spirits that influence people to embrace homosexuality.

Please notice; one of the characteristics of those who depart from the faith in the End Times is FORBIDDING TO MARRY.

Or, we could say it this way: RESISTING GOD'S ESTABLISHED ORDER.

Of course, this would obviously apply to heterosexual couples living together out of wedlock, but also, very definitely, it would apply to *"Gay"* or lesbian couples.

Do not be fooled by the futile attempts of homosexuals to cover up sin by entering into same-sex marriages, and then, insisting that such unions are acceptable, because they are monogamous.

Same-sex marriages violate God's order, which he established in creation.

2) Exchanging the truth of God for lies:

"Therefore God also gave them up to uncleanness, in the lusts of their hearts, to dishonor their bodies among themselves, WHO EXCHANGED THE TRUTH OF GOD FOR THE LIE, and worshiped and served the creature rather than the Creator, who is blessed forever. Amen." (Romans 1:24-25).

Earlier in this chapter, we discovered that homosexuals have changed heterosexuality into homosexuality. Then, we learned that they have listened to the wrong spirit. Now, we also discover that they have exchanged the truth of God's Word for lies.

Listening to the wrong spirit is the under-lying reason why the truth of God's Word is exchanged for lies. However, in our natural, physical surroundings, this exchange of truth for lies would simply involve listening to the lies of men, or women, who are influencing people contrary to the Bible. Consequently, the Bible says...

3) God gave them up, or...God gave them over

"For this reason GOD GAVE THEM UP to vile passions...And even as they did not like to retain God in their knowledge, GOD GAVE THEM OVER to a debased mind...." (from Romans 1:26 & 28).

Did you notice the phrases, GOD GAVE THEM UP, and GOD GAVE THEM OVER? They literally mean: *"God surrendered them, delivered them up, cast them aside, allowed them to be put into prison."*

And, please notice the serious condition to which God gives them up, or gives them over: A DEBASED MIND. Other translations use the phrase: REPROBATE MIND.

The Bible defines debased (reprobate) as: *"Not approved by God; thus rejected."*

Obviously, this is a condition of extreme jeapordy. Whether or not it is irreconcilable, I do not know. God is the judge.

But remember, homosexuals arrive at this condition by listening to seducing, deceiving spirits, and by changing the truth of God's Word for lies!

Before we move to question # 3, allow me to share some insight that the Holy Spirit has imparted to me.

I have been sharing with you, biblical facts as to why a person embraces homosexuality. It is also a fact that other contributing factors lead to a person becoming homosexual.

For example, if we were able to look into the backgrounds of homosexuals, we would often find child molestation. More often than not, we would also discover these ungodly encounters to be forced, not consensual.

Our Heavenly Father is a God of justice; he would not punish the oppressed along with the oppressor. I am convinced that God does not hold a child responsible for sinful acts that were forced upon them.

But, listen carefully to the following…

I heard the testimony of a man who was molested as a child, and forced to engage in homosexual activities. However, as he grew into adulthood, the time came when...

IT WAS AS IF GOD HAD SET BEFORE HIM – TWO ROADS.

One road led to heterosexuality; the other road led to homosexuality.

The temptation to take the homosexual road was very strong. It was the only kind of sexual activity he had ever known.

But also, at these crucial crossroads, he came face to face with the reality that he could no longer blame the events of the past, nor the people of the past, for the road he would chose. From this time forth, he would be accountable to God for his actions.

Because of the fear of God in this man's life, he chose heterosexuality.

The Lord is a God of mercy and grace, as well as a God of judgment. Therefore, I am convinced that every homosexual has faced those two roads.

At that moment of decision, they became accountable to God. Therefore, on the Day of Judgment, they will not have an excuse for their decision, and subsequent lifestyle.

Question # 3 – Can homosexuals be Christians (at the same time)?

In response to this question, let me begin by making a strong emphasis...

A person cannot be a genuine Christian and an AVOWED homosexual at the same time. The two lifestyles just cannot exist together.

AVOWED means to openly confess; thus, to be totally committed to something. Such actions are actually one of the requirements of the Christian faith. Jesus said:

"...whoever confesses Me before men, him I will also confess before My Father who is in heaven. But whoever denies Me before men, him I will also deny before My Father who is in heaven." (Matthew 10:32-33).

Someone who has inherited the kingdom of God – by openly confessing Christ – could not at the same time openly confess to being homosexual, which the Bible clearly says will exclude them from the kingdom of God!

Listen to these additional observations, explanations, and conclusions.

When a person truly accepts Jesus Christ, a powerful transformation takes place in their life. Literally, they pass from death into life.

However, it doesn't take long to discover that some of the sins of the flesh linger on. As examples:

1) The alcoholic who accepts Jesus as Savior may go through a tough period of overcoming alcoholism before he is totally set free.
2) The habitual marijuana smoker who accepts Jesus Christ may experience a great struggle with temptation before he is completely set free.
3) The liar may have to repeatedly cry out to God from Psalm 141:3: *"Set a guard, O Lord, over my mouth; keep watch over the door of my lips,"* before he learns to practice the truth.

Yet, despite the fact that the Christian life is one of growing, and overcoming, we must not overlook the clear description in God's Word of someone who has accepted Jesus Christ. 2 Corinthians 5:17 says:

"Therefore, if anyone is in Christ, he is a new creation; old things have passed away; behold, all things have become new."

Everyone who has truly accepted Jesus Christ will experience change in their lives. They will not continue to live flagrant, sinful, ungodly lifestyles. For example...

1) The thief who accepts Jesus cannot worship God on Sunday, and then, rob banks during the week!
2) The adulterer who gets saved cannot shout and dance in church on Sunday, and have sex with other men's wives during the week! The two lifestyles just do not go together.

Similarly, homosexuals who accept Jesus will likely experience a struggle against those seducing spirits. Soon however, if they have truly accepted the Lord, deliverance will be their testimony.

They cannot be a genuine, born again Christian, and an avowed homosexual at the same time. 1 Corinthians 6:9-10, which we have looked at several times, reminds us of two strong emphases:

God himself gives these warnings:

1) DO NOT BE DECEIVED,
2) HOMOSEXUALS WILL NOT INHERIT THE KINGDOM OF GOD.

Question # 4 – Doesn't God love all of us unconditionally?

Yes, God loves everyone unconditionally, including homosexuals. However, this fact does not mean he APPROVES of everyone unconditionally, and it does not mean he ACCEPTS everyone unconditionally!

In Mark 10:17-22, we find what is often called the story of the rich young ruler. He knelt before Jesus and asked: *"...what shall I do that I may inherit eternal life?"* Jesus answered by telling the young man to keep the commandments.

[NOTE: At this time, Jesus could not tell this man to trust in the shed blood of Christ, because he had not yet died for our sins].

The man insisted that he had kept all the commandments from his youth, but Jesus said to him:

"...One thing you lack: Go your way, sell whatever you have and give to the poor, and you will have treasure in heaven; and come, take up the cross, and follow Me."

The Bible says of this rich young man: *"...he was sad at this word, and went away sorrowful, for he had great possessions."*

Of course, giving to the poor cannot buy our way into Heaven, but this man's wealth was keeping him out of Heaven.

Now, listen to what the Bible says about Jesus as he observed this young man: *"Then Jesus, looking at him, LOVED HIM...."*

Jesus loved this man unconditionally, but he did not approve of him, nor accept him. Jesus did not run after the young man, and say, *"OK, wait, maybe I was a bit too harsh. How about half of your goods to the poor?"*

Similarly, God loves homosexuals, but he will not lower his standards, and approve of homosexuality. Neither will God accept them if they persist in holding on to their current, sinful lifestyle.

Homosexuality will keep a person out of the kingdom of God, and will eventually send them to Hell, but Jesus will still love them, before, during, and after they have made their choice!

Question # 5 – Can homosexuals become born again Christians?

Obviously, the answer is YES, but not without changes taking place in that person's life. 1 Corinthians 6:9-10 clearly states that homosexuals and sodomites will not inherit the kingdom of God, but the very next verse, 1 Corinthians 6:11, says the following:

"And such WERE some of you. But you were washed, but you were sanctified, but you were justified in the name of the Lord Jesus and by the Spirit of our God."

However, homosexuals must come to the Lord the same as every sinner. Specifically, by the WAY OF REPENTANCE:

"From that time Jesus began to preach and to say, REPENT, for the kingdom of heaven is at hand." (Matthew 4:17).

To repent means: *"To change one's mind, or to change one's purpose."* Repentance involves turning to God, but also, it requires TURNING AWAY FROM SIN!

Repentance is not a human effort to clean up one's own life. Ephesians 2:8-9 reveals that salvation is not from man's efforts.

Repentance involves the WILLINGNESS to turn away from sin. Then, if a person truly accepts Jesus Christ, the power of God will begin to set them free from sin.

To the contrary, many people (homosexuals and other sinners) say they believe in Jesus, but they REFUSE TO REPENT. They insist on continuing sinful lifestyles, which the Bible says will separate them from God.

Some of these people may have prayed a so-called sinner's prayer, inviting Jesus into their life. Yet, in their hearts, they have no intention of turning away from sin. Jude, in his short epistle, warned of such people:

"...certain men whose condemnation was written about long ago have secretly slipped in among you. They are godless men, who change the grace of our God into a LICENSE FOR IMMORALITY and deny Jesus Christ our only Sovereign and Lord." (Jude 4 NIV).

Such people could not be genuinely born again. One cannot by-pass repentance, nor ignore repentance when coming to Christ.

Jesus himself warned about repentance:

"There were present at that season some who told Him about the Galileans whose blood Pilate had mingled with their sacrifices. And Jesus answered and said to them, Do you suppose that these Galileans were worse sinners than all other Galileans, because they suffered such things? I tell you, no; but UNLESS YOU REPENT you will all likewise perish. Or those eighteen on whom the tower in Siloam fell and killed them, do you think that they were worse sinners than all other men who dwelt in Jerusalem? I tell you, no; but UNLESS YOU REPENT you will all likewise perish." (Luke 13:1-5).

Homosexuals (and other sinners) are freely invited to receive God's saving grace through Jesus Christ. But remember, the salvation Jesus provides is actually a work of God, SAVING US FROM OUR SINS!

A Challenge to Homosexuals...

Will you admit that from God's viewpoint, homosexuality is sin, and that your lifestyle is separating you from God?

Are you willing to repent before God? Are you willing to turn to God, and turn away from homosexuality?

If so, following is a prayer of repentance, and acceptance of Jesus Christ…

Heavenly Father, thank you for sending Jesus Christ into this world to die for my sins on the cross, and to shed his blood for the remission of my sins.

I repent before you, Lord. I admit that homosexuality is a sinful lifestyle, and it is separating me from you.

Heavenly Father, I believe you raised Jesus from the dead. He is alive now. He can come into my life, and change me into a new person.

Lord Jesus, I believe you are able to set me free from homosexuality. I invite you into my heart. Cleanse me with the blood you shed upon the cross. Give me a right standing before God, the Father.

Thank you, Lord Jesus, that I am now born again. The power of God is at work in my life, freeing me from homosexuality.

From this time forth in my life, I openly confess that you, Jesus, are my Savior, my Lord and my God. Amen.

Chapter Five

Guarding your Children against Homosexual spirits

"Though one may be overpowered by another, two can withstand him. And a THREEFOLD CORD is not quickly broken." (Ecclesiastes 4:12).

In this chapter, I will teach you a threefold defense for guarding your children against the seducing, deceiving spirits that influence people to embrace homosexual lifestyles.

Defense # 1 – Authority in the name of the Lord Jesus Christ over ALL THE POWER of the enemy

Note the following conversation between Jesus and his disciples, and listen carefully to his instructions to them, and to us:

"Then the seventy returned with joy, saying, Lord, even the demons are subject to us IN YOUR NAME. And He said to them, I saw Satan fall like lightning from heaven. Behold, I GIVE YOU THE AUTHORITY to trample on serpents and scorpions, and over all the power of the enemy, and nothing shall by any means hurt you." (Luke 10:17-19).

When Jesus used the words, SERPENTS and SCORPIONS, he was not talking about poisonous snakes that crawl on the ground. He was referring to Satan and demons.

Jesus has given us authority over all the power of the enemy, including authority over the seducing, deceiving spirits that influence people to embrace homosexuality.

72

As I taught you in an earlier chapter, if these evil spirits can deceive our children to believe homosexuality is normal, and tempt them to experiment with *"gay"* or lesbian encounters, then eventually, they may also convince them to embrace the lifestyle.

So, listen carefully on how to employ this first *"Cord of Defense..."*

Christian parents, and everyone who has responsibilities for child rearing (grandparents, foster parents), you must become Watchmen on the Walls on behalf of your children.

If you observe your sons EXHIBITING FEMININE CHARACTERISTICS, speak out loud to those seducing, deceiving spirits, by the authority of the name of Jesus Christ, and command those spirits to loose your sons, and be gone from them!

Now, listen to a caution. Be careful with your observations; do not go on a spiritual witch-hunt. All of our sons will not become rugby players; some of them may become concert violinists.

Learn to depend upon the Holy Spirit. In 1 Corinthians 12:7-11, the Bible speaks of the manifestations (or gifts) of the Holy Spirit. One of those gifts is the DISCERNING OF SPIRITS (knowing what spirits are at work).

If the gift of discerning of spirits does not seem to be operating in your life, then ask God for wisdom to know whether or not evil spirits are at work. James 1:5 says:

"If any of you lacks wisdom, let him ask of God, who gives to all liberally and without reproach, and it will be given to him."

But, hear a further caution. Do not ignore the activity of homosexual spirits, and just hope they will go away. In the coming days, as we progress further into these End Times, the homosexual threat will not decrease; it will increase!

Likewise, Christian parents, and all those responsible for child rearing, if you observe your daughters EXHIBITING MASCULINE CHARACTERISTICS, speak to those spirits in the name of Jesus Christ, and command those evil, seducing spirits to loose your daughters, and be gone from them.

Again, learn to depend upon God's Holy Spirit, or ask God for wisdom. Just because some of our daughters like to climb trees, rather than sitting around all day polishing their fingernails, does not mean they are in danger of becoming lesbians.

But again, let me reemphasize; do not ignore the activity of homosexual spirits!

A Mother's Prayer...

A Christian mother, who is also a pastor, shared the following with me.

When her children were growing up, she regularly employed a specific prayer, which was based upon Matthew 10:26:

"...For there is nothing covered that will not be revealed, and hidden that will not be known."

By employing this prayer, she trusted God to reveal to her, any ungodly influences that might wrongly affect her children.

God was faithful. He consistently showed this mother:
- ✓ Where her children went,
- ✓ What they were doing, and
- ✓ With whom they were hanging around.

I recommend this prayer to all Christian parents. In these increasingly dangerous End Times, we must become Watchmen on the Walls on behalf of our children.

Defense # 2 – Speak protective scriptures into the lives of your children on a regular basis.

When my children were growing up, not many days passed that I did not speak these verses from Psalm 91:10-11 into their lives:

"No evil shall befall you, nor shall any plague come near your dwelling; for He shall give His angels charge over you, to keep you (or guard you) *in all your ways."*

My children became accustomed to this lifestyle. If I forgot to speak these verses into their lives, they would hang around, lean on me, or stare at me until I remembered.

When we speak the word of God, angels go into action to fulfill it.

"Bless the LORD, you His angels, who excel in strength, who do His word, heeding the voice of His word." (Psalm 103:20).

"Are not all angels ministering spirits sent to serve (provide assistance for) *those who will inherit salvation?"* (Hebrews 1:14 NIV).

All those scriptures are good, and you need to use them, but for our second *"Cord of Defense,"* let us focus upon several verses that are especially important for guarding our children against homosexual spirits.

"But You, O LORD, are a shield for me (or, a shield all around me), *my glory and the One who lifts up my head."* (Psalm 3:3).

Listen to a portion of that scripture again: *"You, O Lord, are...THE ONE WHO LIFTS UP MY HEAD."*

The word, HEAD, from my Hebrew study helps, means the following: *"To shake; the head (as most easily shaken), whether literal or figurative."*

Of course, literally speaking, our head, which is designed to easily rotate around our neck, is easily shaken.

Figuratively speaking, the part of us that is most easily shaken is our EMOTIONS, and this is precisely where homosexual spirits will be attacking our children!

A lady came up to me following a service in which I taught a message based upon this chapter. She was finally able to understand how her niece had become a lesbian.

Her niece was comforting a girl friend who was going through a difficult time. She had described to her aunt how she sat with this girl friend, cried with her, and embraced her. *"At that exact moment,"* her niece explained, *"I knew I was a lesbian!"*

This niece mistook emotional concern for sexual love, and thus, made a life changing, eternity threatening decision, based entirely on her emotions.

Our children need the Lord to be a shield for them. God will protect them, lift up their heads, and lift up their countenances, when their emotions are all stirred up.

So, Christian parents, be bold. Look into your children's eyes, and say to them:

The Lord is a shield all around you. He will be your glory; the one in whom you see splendor, the one in whom you find majesty, the one to whom you give honor. The Lord God will lift up your head, he will lift up your countenance, and he will guard your emotions in times of trouble and distress.

Here is another scripture pertaining to the guarding of our children's emotions:

"Why are you cast down, O my soul? And why are you disquieted within me? Hope in God; for I shall yet praise Him, the help of my countenance and my God." (Psalm 43:5).

Look your children in the eyes, and say:

My son (or my daughter) in the name of Jesus Christ, your soul will not be cast down. Your soul will not be disquieted within you. Your hope is in God. Lift up your voice and praise him, and he will be the help of your countenance.

Defense # 3 – Speak Biblical Blessings over your children

In the Bible, we find examples of godly parents speaking spiritual blessings into the lives of their children.

For some reason, Christians have ceased to continue this practice. Maybe we thought such practices were just for the Jews?

Of course, when you think about it, we are the Jews! According to Romans 2:28-29, the real Jews are those who are circumcised in their heart.

So, whether we are Messianic Jews, who are also the physical seed of Abraham, or Gentiles grafted into the vine, we are both the real Jews; the spiritual seed of Abraham. Maybe we should start acting like Jews!

Also, consider the fact that Jesus blessed little children (read Mark 10:13-16), and we will speak more about this in a later chapter.

Our third *"Cord of Defense"* comes in the form of two Old Testament blessings; one for the sons, and one for the daughters.

Hebrews 4:12 reveals that God's Word is living and powerful, and with that in mind, I believe God has shown me the following...

When you lay your hands upon your sons and daughters, and speak these blessings into their lives, the life and power from these Words of God will guard your children from the influences of homosexual spirits.

A Blessing for the sons...

In Genesis, chapter 48, we have the story of Jacob (whose name was changed to Israel) blessing the sons of Joseph. You can read the entire account on your own, but for the sake of this teaching, I have separated the following passages:

80

"God, before whom my fathers Abraham and Isaac walked, the God who has fed me all my life long to this day, the Angel who has redeemed me from all evil, bless the lads; let my name be named upon them, and the name of my fathers Abraham and Isaac; and LET THEM GROW INTO A MULTITUDE in the midst of the earth...So he blessed them that day, saying, By you Israel will bless, saying, may God make you as Ephraim and as Manasseh...." (from verses 15-16, 20).

Please notice the words in capital letters. In blessing the sons of Joseph, Jacob said: *"...LET THEM GROW INTO A MULTITUDE in the midst of the earth...."*

So, how can this blessing from the mouth of Jacob protect our children today from the influences of homosexual spirits?

Think about it; a so-called *"Gay"* relationship between two men cannot grow into a multitude! In fact, they cannot grow at all. Homosexual relationships do not have the capability of producing offspring.

Christian parents; may I encourage you to gather your sons about you, lay your hands upon each of them, and speak the blessing on the following page into their lives:

My Son, in the name of the Lord Jesus Christ, when the time is right, may God bless you with a godly wife, and may God make you as Ephraim and Manasseh, and may you grow into a multitude in the midst of the earth.

A Blessing for the daughters...

In the book of Ruth, we find the blessing for the daughters. As Ruth was preparing to marry Boaz, the Bible says:

"And all the people who were at the gate, and the elders, said, we are witnesses. The LORD make the woman who is coming to your house like Rachel and Leah, the two WHO BUILT THE HOUSE OF ISRAEL; and may you prosper in Ephrathah and be famous in Bethlehem." (Ruth 4:11).

Again, notice the capitalized letters? The Bible says of Rachel and Leah, *"...the two WHO BUILT THE HOUSE OF ISRAEL...."*
So, how could this blessing protect our daughters from homosexual spirits? Simply put, lesbian relationships cannot build any house; they cannot produce offspring.

Christian parents, gather your daughters about you, lay your hands on each of them, and speak this blessing into their lives:

My daughter, in the name of the Lord Jesus Christ, when the time is right, may the Lord bless you with a godly husband, and make you as Rachel and Leah. As they built up the house of Israel, may you give birth to children who will know the Lord, and build up the house of God. May you be blessed to populate Heaven.

Christian parents, I appeal to you; please do not take these matters lightly. Please do not fail to guard your sons and daughters from the seducing, deceiving spirits, which, as we progress further into the End Times, will be increasingly attacking our children.

In conclusion to this chapter, I believe the Lord would have me add the following…

I AM AGAINST VIOLENCE. I am against violence toward any group of people.

In this book, I have taken a strong stance against homosexuality, because the Word of God teaches that it is a sinful lifestyle, and therefore separates people from God.

However, I take an equally strong stance against violence toward homosexuals, sometimes referred to as *"gay bashing."*

As a minister of the Gospel, and a servant of the Lord, I am obligated to teach the Bible in an uncompromising manner, but I would never endorse, nor encourage hate crimes against homosexuals, or any other group of people.

During his earthly ministry, Jesus taught the truth in a bold, straightforward manner, but he did not employ violence as a means of forcing people to submit to his teachings. Jesus was after the hearts of men.

In a similar manner, I am also after the hearts of men. I desire to see homosexuals (as well as other sinners) repent of sin, and truly accept Jesus Christ as Savior and Lord, and subsequently, be delivered from a lifestyle that the Bible says will exclude them from the kingdom of God.

Book Two

Preparing your children to experience the Outpouring of God's Holy Spirit

Prologue

As you have already figured out, this book is primarily written to Christians, and aimed directly at Christian parenting.

Much of what is contained within the book is written under the assumption that you, and your children have accepted the Lord Jesus Christ, and are therefore already born again.

However, I would be negligent if I did not dedicate a portion of the book to instruction on how to be born again, and to do so in a manner that will enable Christian parents to lead their children to Jesus Christ.

Much of what is contained within this book would not even be applicable to our children unless they have truly trusted in the Lord Jesus Christ as their Savior and Lord.

With these thoughts in mind, beginning on the following page, I have laid out a simple, easy to understand format of the essentials in accepting Jesus Christ.

1) Sin separates us from God. Sin can be defined as disobeying God's laws.

   "But your iniquities have separated you from your God; and your sins have hidden His face from you, so that He will not hear." (Isaiah 59:2).

2) Everyone has sinned.

   "For all have sinned and fall short of the glory of God." (Romans 3:23).

3) Someone must pay for sin. Jesus Christ, God's only begotten Son, came into this world to die on the cross, and shed his blood for the forgiveness of our sins.

   "For God so loved the world that He gave His only begotten Son, that whoever believes in Him should not perish but have everlasting life." (John 3:16).

   "Who Himself (Jesus Christ) *bore our sins in His own body on the tree* (on the cross), *that we, having died to sins, might live for righteousness − by whose stripes you were healed."* (1 Peter 2:24).

4) We must repent. Repentance is turning away from sin, and turning to God.

"Repent, then, and turn to God, so that your sins may be wiped out, that times of refreshing may come from the Lord." (Acts 3:19 NIV).

5) We must believe that God, the Heavenly Father, raised his Son, Jesus, from the dead. We must believe Jesus is alive.

"...God raised him from the dead, freeing him from the agony of death, because it was impossible for death to keep its hold on him." (Acts 2:24 NIV).

6) We must invite Jesus Christ into our lives, and trust in his shed blood for forgiveness and cleansing of our sins.

"...who loved us and washed us from our sins in His own blood." (Revelation 1:5).

"But as many as received Him, to them He gave the right to become children of God, to those who believe in His name." (John 1:12).

7) We must confess (tell others) that Jesus Christ is our Lord.

"...if you confess with your mouth, JESUS IS LORD, and believe in your heart that God raised him from the dead, you will be saved." (Romans 10:9 NIV).

After you explain these matters to your children, here is a prayer you can pray with them to accept Jesus Christ:

Heavenly Father, thank you for sending your Son, Jesus Christ, into this world to die for my sins.

I admit that I have sinned. I need to be forgiven, and have my sins washed away.

With your help, O Lord, I repent. I turn away from my sins, and I turn to you, Lord Jesus.

Heavenly Father, I believe you raised Jesus from the dead. He is alive now.

Lord Jesus, I invite you into my life. Please forgive my sins, and wash away my sins with your blood.

From this time forth in my life, Jesus Christ, you are my Lord, and I will tell others about you. Amen.

After your children have accepted Jesus Christ as their Savior, it is very important that they be baptized in water.

Please have your children immersed in baptism, not sprinkled. The word, BAPTIZE, literally means: *"To immerse, to submerge, to make overwhelmed (or make fully wet)."*

The Bible pattern is baptism by immersion (see Mark 1:9-10 and Acts 8:35-38).

Water baptism is important because...

1) Jesus commanded us to be baptized.

> *"Go therefore and make disciples of all the nations, baptizing them in the name of the Father and of the Son and of the Holy Spirit."* (Matthew 28:19).

2) In water baptism, we openly identify with the death, burial, and resurrection of the Lord Jesus Christ.

> *"We were therefore buried with him through baptism into death in order that, just as Christ was raised from the dead through the glory of the Father, we too may live a new life."* (Romans 6:4 NIV).

3) Water baptism helps break the power of sin from our lives.

"For we know that our old self (before we accepted Jesus Christ) *was crucified with him so that the body of sin* (or sinful body) *might be done away with, that we should no longer be slaves to sin – because anyone who has died has been freed from sin."* (Romans 6:6-7 NIV).

Some final thoughts…

Water baptism should not be something parents impose upon their children, either when they are infants, or when they are older. Water baptism should follow faith in Jesus Christ by the individual who is being baptized.

But, think about this; as a parent, it is very important to you, that your children obey you. Even more so, it is very important to our Heavenly Father that we obey him.

God has commanded us to be baptized. Therefore, as quickly as possible, we should explain these matters to our children, and encourage them to be diligent about obeying their Heavenly Father.

Chapter Six

That it may be Well with Them

2 Timothy 3:1-5, one of the places where the Bible tells us about the End Times, says the following: *"But know this, that in the last days PERILOUS TIMES WILL COME...."*

In the Amplified Bible, it says: *"...times of great stress and trouble – hard to deal with and hard to bear...."* In the margin of my NKJV Bible, it says: *"irreconcilable times."*

So, how can we recognize these perilous times? Shall we take a closer look?

Those verses identify certain traits we can expect to see in these perilous End Times:

▶**Men will be lovers of themselves** ▶**lovers of money** ▶**boasters** ▶**proud** ▶**blasphemers** ▶**disobedient to parents** ▶**unthankful** ▶**unholy** ▶**unloving** ▶**unforgiving** ▶**slanderers** ▶**without self-control** ▶**brutal** ▶**despisers of good** ▶**traitors** ▶**headstrong** ▶**haughty** ▶**lovers of pleasure rather than lovers of God** ▶**having a form of godliness but denying its power.**

Of course, one would expect blasphemy, a lack of holiness, brutality, and betrayal to characterize the perilous End Times, but did you notice DISOBEDIENCE TO PARENTS was also in the list?

Christian parents; in these dangerous End Times, please do not ignore this problem.

➢ Please, do not justify disobedience by explaining that it's the natural tendency of a strong-willed child.

➢ Please, do not overlook disobedience, assuming that it's just a passing little temper tantrum.

➢ Please, do not dismiss disobedience as just a maturing child expressing his or her independence.

Yes, parents must deal with all these traits during child rearing, but please come to an understanding that disobedience to parents is also a sign of the perilous times that are now coming upon the whole earth.

Let me make an even stronger emphasis. Both you and your children need to clearly understand the following…

The attitudes and actions described in the previous list (from 2 Timothy, chapter 3) are the very tools Satan is using to usher unsuspecting souls into an eternal hell.

Lest you think I'm exaggerating, let me once again draw your attention to the Word of God. In Romans 1:28, the Bible says:

"And even as they did not like to retain God in their knowledge, God gave them over to a DEBASED MIND, to do those things which are not fitting."

In chapter four we talked about the phrase DEBASED MIND (also known as a REPROBATE MIND). As a reminder, this phrase actually means: *"Those whom God cannot approve of; thus, he rejects.*

In chapter four, we were focusing upon God's disapproval and eventual rejection of homosexuals, who refuse to repent.

So, what else could cause the God of all grace and mercy to turn someone over to a debased mind? From Romans 1:29-31, listen to a list of attitudes and actions similar to the list in 2 Timothy, chapter 3:

►Being filled with all unrighteousness ►sexual immorality ►wickedness ►covetousness ►maliciousness ►full of envy ►murder ►strife ►deceit ►evil-mindedness ►they are whisperers ►backbiters ►haters of God ►violent ►proud ►boasters ►inventors of evil things ►disobedient to parents ►undiscerning ►untrustworthy ►unloving ►unforgiving ►un-merciful.

Of course, you obviously took note of the fact that disobedience to parents is in this list also! And, did you realize that disobedience to parents is unrighteousness?

No, children will not automatically go to Hell if they disobey their parents. Teaching obedience is part of parenting. Yet, we must understand that rebellion against parental authority is the same attitude that eventually results in rebellion against God's authority.

Now, listen to a word of caution. Don't try to teach these things to your children during one of those shouting matches between you and them.

Set aside some quality time, look your children straight in the eyes, tell them God loves them, tell them you love them, then instruct them in the truth of God's Word.

Equally important, you need to emphasize that the Lord really appreciates children who obey their parents. So much so, that he has made them some significant promises!

From the eternal, unchanging, totally true Word of God, we read the following:

"Children, obey your parents in the Lord, for this is right. Honor your father and mother, which is the first commandment WITH PROMISE: that it may be well with you, and you may live long on the earth." (Ephesians 6:1-3).

Did you notice what our Heavenly Father promises to those children who are obedient to their parents?

1) It will be well with them.
2) They will live long on the earth.

I should also point out that this scriptural principle originally appears in Exodus 20:12, as part of The Ten Commandments.

These are the same Ten Commandments that unrighteous people are fighting against, and seeking to have banned from our public places and schools.

It baffles the mind to realize that grown people are actually against children obeying their parents! I think you can clearly see why perilous times are upon us.

Please also notice that the Word of God emphasizes: *"...children, obey your parents IN THE LORD...."* Obviously, the Lord would not hold a child responsible for disobeying ungodly parents, especially those who were requiring their children to participate in sinful activities. God is not a child abuser!

But, equally important, God is not against child discipline. The Bible so instructs us:

"Foolishness is bound up in the heart of a child; the ROD OF CORRECTION (or staff, as a shepherd's staff) *will drive it far from him."* (Proverbs 22:15).

And, why is child discipline so important? Listen to the following verses:

"Do not withhold correction from a child, for if you beat him with a rod, he will not die. You shall beat him with a rod, and deliver his soul from hell." (Proverbs 23:13-14).

Do not close your ears to the above words of instruction. I have already stated that God is not a child abuser. Yet, from God's viewpoint, child discipline (including spanking) is still acceptable, not just to insure obedience from your children, but also, TO DELIVER THEIR SOUL FROM HELL!

Again, we can see that rebellion against parental authority will later manifest itself in rebellion against God's authority.

Well, let's again focus on God's promises. Christian parents, has the following truth of God's Word penetrated your heart...?

God actually guarantees the well-being and long life of your children, if they will simply obey you!

A pastor friend shared about attending a missionary conference. Another attendee at the conference was a minister who was over 100 years old.

This aged servant of God was not brought to the conference in an ambulance, nor did he attend the sessions in a wheelchair.

He was in excellent health, with a sound mind, walking around and fellowshipping with the other attendees.

When it was discovered how old he was, he was asked to share the secret of his longevity. I don't know exactly how things happened, but very possibly, the conference schedule was altered in order to give this elderly minister a time slot.

I can just imagine the people getting out their Bibles and notebooks, preparing for some in-depth teaching.

This servant of God got up, and simply stated, *"I OBEYED MY PARENTS."* Then, he sat back down!

I sincerely believe God intends to pour out his Spirit on this generation (and succeeding generations) of children and young people, but the outpouring will not be upon the rebellious and disobedient.

Christian parents, God's intentions toward our children are clearly stated: THAT IT MAY BE WELL WITH THEM, but you also have a responsibility!

Chapter Seven

Sitting at the Feet of Jesus

"Now it happened as they went that He entered a certain village; and a certain woman named Martha welcomed Him into her house. And she had a sister called Mary, who also sat at Jesus' feet and heard His word. But MARTHA WAS DISTRACTED with much serving, and she approached Him and said,

Scriptures continued, next page...

101

...Lord, do You not care that my sister has left me to serve alone? Therefore tell her to help me. And Jesus answered and said to her, Martha, Martha, YOU ARE WORRIED AND TROUBLED ABOUT MANY THINGS. But one thing is needed, and Mary has chosen that good part, which will not be taken away from her." (Luke 10:38-42).

Today's world, at least in America and other so-called developed countries, is a fast paced, high-energy society. The fruit of such an environment is not always good.

When one observes the children of this high-energy environment, they discover that many children have great difficulty just sitting quietly.

Many children cannot sit quietly in a classroom, and complete their schoolwork. They are constantly distracted, fail to perform their own work, and disrupt others in the class.

Many children cannot even sit quietly in an automobile while being transported from place to place. They must have some type of electronic toy to fill every second.

And, today's children are quickly bored, always demanding to have the latest gadget, with the newest technology.

I feel sorry for today's teen-agers who are seeking Summer jobs, or part-time employment. Very likely, they will be fired unless they scurry about like a bantam rooster.

Employers don't seem to be interested in attributes like faithfulness and honesty. They just want employees to be the high-energy types, who run around with plastic smiles on their faces, exhibiting fake enthusiasm.

Advertising agencies aggressively employ high-energy techniques. Images flash upon our television screens in rapid succession, often leaving one wondering what exactly is being advertised.

And, let's not slight the toy manufacturers. They have saturated our society with vivid, fast paced, vicious video games.

Today's child can spend countless hours on the Internet, supposedly doing research for school projects, but all too often delving into ungodly websites.

When I was a child, the word, STRESS, was not even a part of our vocabulary. Today, third graders are receiving counseling because of stress.

And, we would be appalled if we knew the number of children that are on so-called, mood altering medications.

It has been suggested that a major cause of stress is TOO MANY CHOICES.

Perhaps it could best be said in another way, TOO MANY DISTRACTIONS.

Interestingly, in the opening scriptures of this chapter, we have a similar situation in the biblical story of Martha and Mary.

Martha was apparently the high-energy, fast paced type, whom the Bible says was DISTRACTED by much serving. Jesus also said she was WORRIED and TROUBLED about many things.

Mary, on the other hand, sat quietly at the feet of Jesus, listening to his words. Please notice that Jesus described Mary's actions as CHOOSING THE GOOD PART.

And, please notice how Jesus responded to Martha's anxieties when she complained: *"...Lord, do You not care that my sister has left me to serve alone...?"*

Jesus said to Martha, and forever alerted everyone who has ears to hear: *"...Mary has chosen that good part, which will not be TAKEN AWAY from her."*

Now, don't misunderstand. An attitude of serving is a desirable trait, but it should never preempt sitting at the feet of Jesus!

I am convinced that much of today's fast paced, high-energy environment is a clever scheme, engineered by the devil himself; a deceptive scheme aimed at DISTRACTING OUR CHILDREN.

Being more specific, a scheme designed to TAKE AWAY THE GOOD PART, so they won't have any quiet time to sit at the feet of Jesus, and listen to his word.

Of course, Jesus is not here in the flesh, so the children cannot literally and physically sit at his feet. However, they can sit at the feet of godly parents, godly grandparents, and godly teachers.

Again, parents must become Watchmen on the Walls on behalf of their children, and here are some of the challenges...

FIRST: Do not allow yourself to become too busy, or too caught up in this fast paced, high-energy environment, that you simply NEGLECT THE GOOD PART.

In today's world, parents and children can get caught up in GOOD THINGS, and still neglect the GOOD PART. I am talking about running the children all over town for school activities, soccer practice, language classes, piano lessons, shopping at the Mall, etc.

SECOND: We must not just tell our kids what to do. We must demonstrate to them, and participate with them, that the good part of life is sitting at the feet of Jesus.

THIRD: We must be on the alert to guard our children from the stress and distractions of this high-energy society, lest the good part BE TAKEN AWAY FROM THEM.

Be assured that Satan is working hard to steal that good part. Indeed, it may already be necessary to re-educate your children, to convince them of the value of a quiet time!

Parents often say their children just need a lot of hugs and kisses. Yes, this is true, but they also need to be diligently instructed in the Word of God. In Deuteronomy 6:6-7, Moses spoke about the commandments of God, and said to the parents:

"You shall teach them diligently to your children, and shall talk of them when you sit in your house, when you walk by the way, when you lie down, and when you rise up."

"The work of righteousness will be peace, and the effect of righteousness, QUIETNESS and assurance forever." (Isaiah 32:17).

Chapter Eight

Faithful in what is Least

"He who is faithful in what is least is faithful also in much; and he who is unjust in what is least is unjust also in much." (Luke 16:10).

When I was serving in a pastoral role, and involved in quite a lot of counseling, I would often encourage parents to teach scriptural principles to their children while they were young.

I can still remember the surprised look on one mother's face, and her quick response: *"Oh, that's not important now,"* she declared; *"they will have time to learn those things when they are older."*

Unfortunately, children who are not taught to obey scriptural principles while they are young, are not likely to obey them when they are older.

From my own personal experiences in the arena of child rearing, allow me to share with you, three areas where I taught my children to be FAITHFUL IN WHAT IS LEAST.

Tithes and Offerings

When my children were very young, even before they started school, I would give them an allowance of maybe a dollar. I purposely gave it to them in small coins, then I would have them set aside a dime, and explain that it was the Lord's tithe.

I would further explain that the tithe does not belong to us; it belongs to the Lord, and we should always give it to the Lord's work.

I would also explain that they could give an offering to the Lord (in addition to the tithe), if they wanted to.

If they received money for their birthday, or Christmas, or even if they found money on the ground, I taught them to honor God with his tithe, and with their offerings.

On Sundays, they would drop the Lord's tithe into the offering plate, more than once missing the entire plate. Sometimes, without my prompting, I would see an extra nickel or dime dropped into the plate.

Once, while attending a Bible conference, my oldest daughter (maybe five years old at the time) gave a very small offering to a very large ministry. The ministry sent her a form letter, profusely thanking her for the offering.

Of course, my daughter's tiny offering did not make or break their ministry budget, but their letter highly impressed her.

Now that she is grown, and working, and making quite a bit more money than those early allowances, it's not hard for her to obey God. She was taught to be faithful in what is least. Now, she is faithful in what is much.

Prayer

I remember another time when one of my daughters was complaining about not having any balloons.

Of course, we could have easily solved the matter by purchasing a few balloons the next time we went shopping. Instead, we took advantage of the situation to teach my daughter to apply her faith in God's word.

We guided her in applying basic principles of childlike faith, probably from scriptures like John 16:23-24 and Mark 11:24:

1) Pray to your Heavenly Father in the name of Jesus Christ,
2) Whatever you ask in the name of the Lord Jesus, the Father will give you, that your joy might be full,
3) But, you must believe you receive the balloons when you pray.

Well, pretty soon, we were overcome with balloons! A lady at our church, who was not aware of my daughter's prayer, gave her a whole bag of balloons.

I conducted a wedding, at which were a large number of Mylar, helium filled balloons. After the wedding, the person in charge gave my daughter all the balloons she could carry.

Another time, my daughter awakened one morning to discover a helium filled balloon in her closet. To this day, she says an angel put it there.

Don't wait until your children are grown, and facing life and death situations, before you try to teach them the prayer of faith. By that time, it may be too late! Remember, in his teachings, Jesus himself emphasized the importance of childlike faith.

Church Attendance

When our children were small, I was just beginning my ministry. The church for which I worked had services, revivals, and special events going on all the time. Barbara and I were in church almost every time the doors opened, and our children were there too!

Occasionally, well-meaning people would question the wisdom of dragging our kids to every meeting. *"We don't want to turn our children against God,"* they would explain.

Well, after many years of ministry, I have had the unique opportunity of watching many children of the saints grow up. The results are rather revealing.

There are exceptions, but for the most part, children who were taught at an early age to be faithful in church attendance, are still attending church, and serving God with their lives.

And, what about those children who were allowed to stay home during church services and do homework (supposedly), or stay home and watch television? For the most part, they are still staying at home, watching TV instead of attending church, and they are not serving God with their lives.

My children did not have a great deal of responsibility in those early days at church. Basically, they were required to BE THERE, and BE QUIET.

You see, faithfulness is a biblical principle that guarantees specific results from God. From the parable of the talents in Matthew 25:21, Jesus explained the principle:

"...Well done, good and faithful servant! You have been FAITHFUL WITH A FEW THINGS; I will put you IN CHARGE OF MANY THINGS...." (NIV).

If you teach your children to be faithful in SMALL spiritual responsibilities, be assured that when the time comes, they will also be faithful in LARGE spiritual responsibilities!

And, faithfulness will carry over into other areas of their lives, helping them to achieve success in whatever God calls them to do!

Chapter Nine

No Shame

"...Anyone who trusts in him will never be PUT TO SHAME (dishonored, disgraced, put to the blush). *For there is no difference between Jew and Gentile – the same Lord is Lord of all and richly blesses all who call on him, for, everyone who calls on the name of the Lord will be saved."* (Romans 10:11-13 NIV).

Christian parents, you may not yet realize this fact, but shame is one of the strongest enemies your children face.

Once, I was blessed to hear an excellent teaching on freedom from shame. Throughout the series of messages, the victory cry was, *"SHAME OFF YOU,"* rather than the usual, *"SHAME ON YOU."*

Think about it...

Children are ashamed if they don't have the latest designer clothes; ashamed if they have a bump on their face; ashamed if their teeth are crooked, and ashamed if their hair looks funny.

Short children are ashamed that they are not tall. Tall children are ashamed that they are too tall. Heavy children are ashamed that they are too fat, and sometimes, skinny children (especially the girls) are ashamed that they are not skinny enough.

Young boys entering into adolescence are ashamed because they don't meet up to the standards of the popular, or the athletic.

Similarly, young girls feel shame if they don't have a so-called perfect body, or even if they don't have blonde hair!

We could go on and on, writing an entire book on why our children and young people are constantly bombarded by the agony of, *"SHAME ON YOU,"* rather than the freedom of, *"SHAME OFF YOU."*

The Shame Monger

The real culprit in this, *"SHAME ON YOU"* society is none other than Satan himself.

Now, the devil is not just trying to prevent your kids from having designer blue jeans. He has a much larger objective in mind...

Satan is hard at work, behind a shroud of deception, ultimately trying to cause your children to be ashamed of Jesus.

Looking back to my childhood, when the subject of Jesus Christ would be brought up on the school playground, often in a mocking manner, I can still remember feeling shame, my face feeling all flushed.

The question is, why would the subject of Jesus Christ cause someone to feel shame? It's the shame monger at work, the accuser of the brethren, who goes about to deceive the whole world (see Revelation 12:9-10).

Now, I must admit, during my childhood, because of peer pressure, there were times that I yielded to the shame monger. I was ashamed of Jesus. Remember, our opening verses say: *"...Anyone who trusts in him will never be put to shame..."* (or, put to the blush).

In John, chapter 6, the Bible reveals that many of Jesus' disciples turned back and did not follow him anymore, because his words were difficult to understand.

Jesus said to his twelve original disciples, *"...Do you also want to go away?"*

Peter's reply revealed just how stupid it is to be ashamed of Jesus Christ: *"Lord, to whom shall we go? You have the words of eternal life."* (see John 6:60, 66-69).

Consider the following statement...

I wonder how many adults have failed to answer the call of God upon their lives, because of thought patterns of shame left over from their childhood?

I am talking about thought patterns that Satan cleverly inserts into the minds of our children, convincing them: *"You can't do that; you will fail, you will be embarrassed, people will think you are stupid!"*

Would you not rather have your children thinking: *"I can do all things through Christ who strengthens me?"* (Philippians 4:13).

Somehow, parents must instill within their children, the same attitude as the Apostle Paul, when he boldly and openly declared:

"For I AM NOT ASHAMED of the gospel of Christ, for it is the power of God to salvation for everyone who believes, for the Jew first and also for the Greek" (or Gentiles). (Romans 1:16).

So, the question is, how can we instill boldness and confidence within our children, and deliver them from the shame monger?

Let us begin with a few, simple definitions of the word, SHAME…

1) A feeling of fear that prevents you from doing something.
2) A feeling of fear, because you have already done something.
3) A feeling of fear, because of what you perceive others will think about it.

Now, let me share with you, five keys for guarding your children from shame.

FIRST: In a bold, straightforward manner, explain to your children that SATAN IS THE SOURCE OF SHAME.

Regardless of what they are experiencing, the true source of shame is not their siblings, not their cousins, not their schoolmates, not the other kids in the neighborhood.

SECOND: Clearly teach your children that Satan's ultimate goal is not to embarrass them in front of their peers, but to cause them to be ashamed of Jesus Christ, so they will not accept him as their Savior, nor serve God with their lives.

THIRD: Be on guard; listen carefully to the words coming forth from your children's mouths. Learn to recognize expressions of shame, which are in fact, wrongful intrusions into their minds.

Teach your children to replace thoughts of shame with promises from the Word of God. One promise that I constantly kept before my children was Jeremiah 29:11:

"For I know the plans I have for you, declares the LORD, plans to prosper you and not to harm you, plans to give you hope and a future." (NIV).

FOURTH: Early in their lives, have your children memorize 1 John 1:9:

"If we confess our sins, He is faithful and just to forgive us our sins and to cleanse us from all unrighteousness."

To those who are sensitive toward God, sin actually causes shame. So, early in their lives, teach your children how to apply this scriptural principle. Teach them to QUICKLY and HONESTLY confess their sins to God, and by faith, receive his forgiveness.

FIFTH: Start early, while your children are young, and teach them to be bold about their faith in God. If they are no longer young, start anyway. Don't just preach to them; you set the example! Proverbs 28:1 says:

"The wicked flee when no one pursues, but the righteous are bold as a lion."

I am both pleased and impressed when I hear Christian athletes giving glory to God for their success on the gridiron, basketball court, playing field, etc.

I am just as impressed when I hear young people giving glory to God for helping them achieve academically in their schoolwork.

I am even more impressed when I hear young people declaring that they will not be involved in pre-marital sex, but will wait for that special person, whom God has hand-picked to become their spouse.

Very likely, someone taught them, as a child, to be bold as a lion about their faith in God. Probably, godly parents watched over them, and guarded them from the attacks of the shame monger!

Christian parents, if you will…

✓ Teach your children the Word of God,
✓ Teach them that God is the solution to their problems,
✓ Teach them to quickly and eagerly trust God for everything, and
✓ Teach them to expect God to answer when they pray,

then I can promise you they will have quite a different outlook on life.

Rather than shame, their lives will reflect the words of Psalm 34:5:

"They looked to Him and were RADIANT, and their faces were not ashamed."

Chapter Ten

Bless The Little Children

"Then they brought little children to Him, that He might touch them; but the disciples rebuked those who brought them. But when Jesus saw it, He was greatly displeased and said to them, let the little children come to Me, and do not forbid them; for of such is the kingdom of God. Assuredly, I say to you, whoever does not receive the kingdom of God as a little child will by no means enter it.

Scriptures continued, next page…

...And He took them up in His arms, laid His hands on them, and blessed them." (Mark 10:13-16).

Our opening scriptures in this chapter are frequently misunderstood.

Some have taken liberty with God's Word, suggesting that Jesus took the children up in his arms, sprinkled water on their heads, and thus, baptized them.

Others have imagined that the Lord just gave the little children a hug, patted them on the rump, and sent them on their way.

Shall we take a deeper look?

FIRST: Please recognize that Jesus was GREATLY DISPLEASED when the disciples prevented the children from coming to him.

All too often, we banish the children to the church basement, charge the teenagers to watch over them, and then, we adults can have revival upstairs!

If the children have their own, separate, ANOINTED children's services, that's great. Otherwise, they should be included in the adult services. And, they should be taught to honor and respect God, and thus, behave appropriately in church.

SECOND: Our opening scriptures reveal that Jesus took the little children up in his arms (which obviously meant he already had his hands upon them).

Yet, in two, separate, deliberate actions, the Bible also reveals that Jesus:

1) Laid his hands on them, and...
2) Blessed them.

"And He took them up in His arms, put His hands on them, and blessed them." (Mark 10:16).

One of the elementary principles of the doctrine of Christ is the laying on of hands:

"Therefore let us leave the elementary teachings about Christ and go on to maturity, not laying again the foundation of repentance from acts that lead to death, and of faith in God, instruction about baptisms, the laying on of hands, the resurrection of the dead, and eternal judgment. And God permitting, we will do so." (Hebrews 6:1-3 NIV).

Some have wrongly thought that in order to be mature, we were supposed to abandon these principles. Please take another look!

The word, LEAVE, in the previous verses could not mean to disregard the elementary teachings about Christ. They are part of our foundation. As an example, we should never abandon FAITH IN GOD!

However, it should not be necessary to teach these principles over and over again, every Sunday, to the same group of people, always laying again the same foundation.

In a church that has already established a strong foundation, the people should not only know the elementary principles, they should be USING THEM.

Now, back to our subject. Judging from scriptural examples where the laying on of hands was employed, I believe we can safely conclude that Jesus laid his hands upon the children for the purpose of IMPARTATION. As examples, listen to these verses:

"For I long to see you, that I may IMPART to you some spiritual gift, so that you may be established." (Romans 1:11).

"Do not neglect the gift that is in you, which was GIVEN TO YOU by prophecy with the laying on of the hands of the eldership." (1 Timothy 4:14).

THIRD: After laying his hands on the little children, Mark 10:16 says Jesus BLESSED them. This word, BLESSED, means:

1) To speak well of, or...
2) To speak a benefit into someone's life.

Again, judging from biblical definitions, we can clearly see that speaking a blessing into someone's life was also for the purpose of IMPARTATION.

1 Timothy 4:14, the scripture used on the previous page, mentions both the laying on of hands and the speaking forth of benefits:

"Do not neglect the gift that is in you, which was given to you by PROPHECY with THE LAYING ON OF THE HANDS of the eldership."

Therefore, judging from the scriptures, it is obvious that when Jesus took the children up in his arms, PUT HIS HANDS ON THEM, and BLESSED THEM, that he did so for the purpose of impartation.

In fact, I believe we can safely conclude that Jesus PROPHESIED into the lives of the little children. No wonder the parents wanted to bring their children to Jesus!

Now, here is my point; Jesus said to his disciples, and to us:

"...he who believes in Me, the works that I do he will do also; and greater works than these he will do, because I go to My Father." (John 14:12).

Those who believe in Jesus are supposed to do the works Jesus did. Since Jesus took little children up in his arms, laid his hands on them, and blessed them, so should we!

Instructions for Godly Parents (Grandparents also)

We are living during the last days when God is pouring out his Spirit upon all flesh:

"And it shall come to pass in the last days, says God, that I will pour out of My Spirit on all flesh; your sons and your daughters shall prophesy, your young men shall see visions, your old men shall dream dreams. And on My menservants and on My maidservants I will pour out My Spirit in those days; and THEY SHALL PROPHESY." (Acts 2:17-18).

Lay your hands upon your children, upon your grandchildren, or upon any child with whom you have a relationship, and begin to pray for them. And, pray with expectations!

Who knows, maybe the Spirit of God will give you prophetic utterances to speak into their lives. Utterances perhaps, that pertain to God's plans and purposes for their lives.

Be careful to wait upon the Lord. Do not speak from your own personal preferences for the children, or out of your own personal frustrations about the children!

Additional instructions for Godly Parents

Take your children to church services or meetings where servants of God, who have a prophetic anointing, are ministering.

Now, I realize that in such settings, the person who is ministering may not normally call out little children to prophesy over them.

No problem! Wait until the service is over, take your children by the hand, march up to the front, and say to the servant of God, *"Would you please lay your hands upon my children, and pray over them?"*

Who knows, maybe the Spirit of God will grant prophetic utterances to the servants of God. Utterances perhaps, that could shape the remainder of your children's lives. Even if they just get prayed for, it won't hurt them.

Remember, one of the things Jesus did was BLESS THE LITTLE CHILDREN, and before he ascended into heaven, he said to his disciples, and to us:

"...As the Father has sent Me, I also send you." (John 20:21).

In conclusion, it is not likely that God will give you prophetic utterances every time you pray for your children. So, here are some blessings, straight from God's written Word, that you can freely speak into their lives:

"All your children shall be taught by the LORD, and great shall be the peace of your children." (Isaiah 54:13).

"The LORD bless you and keep you; the LORD make His face shine upon you, and be gracious to you; the LORD lift up His countenance upon you, and give you peace." (Numbers 6:24-26).

Chapter Eleven

Baptized with the Holy Spirit

"...they were all filled with the Holy Spirit and began to speak with other tongues, as the Spirit gave them utterance...the promise is to you and TO YOUR CHILDREN, and to all who are afar off, as many as the Lord our God will call." (Acts 2:4, 39).

In the second chapter of Acts, there are many promises that await those who receive Jesus Christ as Savior. One such promise is to be baptized with the Holy Spirit.

Please notice; the promise to be baptized with the Holy Spirit is not just for the adults, but also for the children!

The word, CHILDREN, used in Acts 2:39 literally means: *"A child."* Figuratively, the word can refer to descendants, but also, very clearly, it simply refers to our own sons and daughters.

The promise to be baptized with the Holy Spirit is to your children, and I am not talking about after they become adults.

I grew up in a church that was opposed to the Holy Spirit baptism. We believed such experiences were just for the early church. We taught that such things had either been withdrawn by God, or had just passed away after the original apostles died.

As a result, we were strongly opposed to any modern day manifestations, or gifts of the Holy Spirit. We were especially opposed to speaking in tongues, even to the extent of declaring that such manifestations were of the devil.

None of these oppositions were based on biblical foundations, but rather, were based on church doctrines, man's interpretations of the scriptures, and even fear.

In 1976, when I received the baptism with the Holy Spirit, it was as if someone turned on the lights in my house. Suddenly, I could see clearly why Satan has fought so hard against this experience…

Satan does not want God's people to receive power in their lives!

Jesus said in Acts 1:8:

"But you shall receive power when the Holy Spirit has come upon you; and you shall be witnesses to Me in Jerusalem, and in all Judea and Samaria, and to the end of the earth."

Although I had already accepted Jesus Christ as Savior, I had no power in my life prior to being baptized with the Holy Spirit. There were certain sins that had a hook in my nose (figuratively speaking), and those sins led me wherever Satan desired.

The power I received from being baptized with the Holy Spirit enabled me to overcome those sins, and shortly thereafter, propelled me into a life of full-time ministry for the Lord Jesus Christ.

There is no way this experience could be from the devil. Satan does not want people to overcome sin, and he definitely does not want people to enter the ministry, and serve God with their lives.

One especially strong benefit that comes from being baptized with the Holy Spirit is the God given ability to speak with other tongues as the Holy Spirit provides the utterance (also known as praying in the Spirit – 1 Corinthians 14:2).

Shortly after being baptized with the Holy Spirit, I came to the realization that speaking with tongues is a means by which GOD'S POWER IS RELEASED in our lives.

"He who speaks in a tongue EDIFIES HIMSELF, but he who prophesies edifies the church." (1 Corinthians 14:4).

The word, EDIFY, means: *"To build up."* Plainly speaking, we could accurately say the word means: TO STRENGTHEN. When we speak with other tongues, we spiritually strengthen ourselves.

I remember sharing these things with a certain youth pastor. At the time, he was not interested in speaking with tongues.

He emphasized that speaking in tongues was for self-edification, and nobly declared that he wanted to concentrate on edifying the church. Unfortunately, this young pastor did not understand self-edification. He thought it meant SELFISHNESS.

There is nothing selfish about speaking in tongues. It is a wonderful gift of God, which enables us to spiritually strengthen ourselves in times of weakness.

And, as for this youth pastor's misguided concept of edifying the church, rather than edifying self; how can we strengthen others, unless we first strengthen ourselves?

Now, perhaps you are wondering, *"Where is all this leading, and how does this apply to our children?"*

In these unstable, increasingly deceptive, incitingly dangerous End Times, our children need the capability to spiritually strengthen themselves!

Very possibly, never before in the history of mankind, have our children been exposed to more temptation, ungodly peer pressure, false teaching, and danger. Indeed, in these last days, there is no longer any such thing as an innocent child.

Thank God for parents who are available to encourage, strengthen, and pray for their children when they come home from school. Unfortunately, in this fast paced, overly busy society, parents are not always available.

And, what about our young people who have gone off to universities? Never before have they faced such blasphemous teaching, sexual looseness, rebellion against authority, and ungodly, alternative lifestyles.

I realize that on many college campuses, Christian organizations conduct Bible studies and prayer groups, but those meetings do not convene but once, maybe twice a week.

What about the in-between times; those times when almost everyone in the dorm has made the decision to go out and get drunk?

Our children and young people need the God-given capability to spiritually strengthen themselves during times of temptation, times of weakness, and even when they are afraid!

And, the Lord has provided that capability through the infilling of his Holy Spirit, and the manifestation of speaking with tongues.

It is well past time for the entire body of Christ to cast aside those tired, old, biblically unfounded doctrines that are opposed to the baptism with the Holy Spirit.

It is time for the entire body of Christ to stop viewing this powerful, vitally important, God-imparted experience, as though it were questionable, or embarrassing.

It is time for the entire body of Christ to eagerly embrace the fullness of God's Holy Spirit, and desire to receive everything that comes with that fullness.

It is time for our children, and our young people to be baptized with the Holy Spirit, and have the capability to pray in the Spirit, and spiritually strengthen themselves to face each new day, and every new challenge.

"But you, beloved, building yourselves up on your most holy faith, praying in the Holy Spirit." (Jude 20).

Obviously, children should also be taught to honor and respect the gifts of God, and not flaunt them in front of their friends. At the same time, they should be taught not to be ashamed of spiritual gifts.

Once your children are baptized with the Holy Spirit, they should also be encouraged to regularly pray in the Spirit as a means of personal, private communion between them and their Heavenly Father.

Praying for your children to be baptized with the Holy Spirit

FIRST: Make sure your children are born again. Only those who have truly accepted Jesus Christ qualify to be baptized with the Holy Spirit.

On pages 87-90, there are instructions for receiving Jesus Christ. If necessary, return to that section, and pray with your children to accept Jesus Christ.

SECOND: From my observations through many years of ministry, only those who are THIRSTY (who desire to experience more of God) will receive the baptism with the Holy Spirit.

Listen to these words spoken by Jesus, as recorded in John 7:37-39:

"On the last day, that great day of the feast, Jesus stood and cried out, saying, IF ANYONE THIRSTS, let him come to Me and drink. He who believes in Me, as the Scripture has said, out of his heart (innermost being) *will flow rivers of living water. But this He spoke concerning the Spirit, whom those believing in Him would receive...."*

THIRD: At the appropriate time, pray with your children. Ask our Heavenly Father, in the name of the Lord Jesus Christ, to baptize them with his Holy Spirit.

"If you then, being evil (or hurtful) *know how to give good gifts to your children, how much more will your heavenly Father give the Holy Spirit to those who ask Him!"* (Luke 11:13).

FOURTH: Before praying, explain to them that they must believe their Heavenly Father will baptize them with his Holy Spirit.

DO NOT MAKE BELIEVING DIFFICULT. Go back to Luke 11:13, and simply ask your children: *"When Jesus said the Father will give the Holy Spirit to those who ask him…*
✓ *DID HE LIE, or*
✓ *DID HE TELL THE TRUTH?"*

"And whatever things you ask in prayer, believing, you will receive." (Matthew 21:22).

FIFTH: Acts 2:4 says the Holy Spirit gave UTTERANCE to those early disciples, and he will also give utterance to your children. However, before praying, explain to them a clear understanding of the word, utterance.

Do not confuse the issue. Utterance is simply unknown words, which the Holy Spirit will give them. Even more simple, utterance is just SOUNDS.

The sounds will not come from their mind, nor will they be audible. John 7:38, from the KJV says: *"...out of his BELLY shall flow rivers of living water."*

After clearly teaching these things, gather your children about you, and pray:

Heavenly Father, in the name of Jesus Christ, please baptize my children with your Holy Spirit.

After praying, lay your hands upon your children, and declare:

Child of God, in the name of Jesus Christ, be filled with God's Holy Spirit!

Encourage them to step out in faith, and speak forth the SOUNDS the Holy Spirit is giving them. You pray along with them.

From this time forth in their lives, they can freely pray in the Spirit whenever they are in need of spiritual strengthening.

Other Books by Jack Michael

Deception In The End Times   (retail) $7.00

"What will be the sign of your coming, and of the end of the age?" When the disciples asked Jesus this question, his immediate response revealed a subject area that is seldom mentioned by end time prophecy teachers.

"And Jesus answered and said to them: Take heed that no one deceives you!"

I am convinced that DECEPTION, at an accelerated pace, will be the primary sign pointing to the return of Christ. And, much of that deception will be aimed directly at the church.

It is with these thoughts in mind, that I present to you, A COMMON SENSE HANDBOOK FOR DISCERNING THE SIGNS OF THE TIMES.

The Best Way To Know God's Will   (retail) $5.00

Have you ever had wishful thoughts that God would leave Heaven for a little while, come down to earth, lead us about by the hand, and show us his will firsthand?

If so, there is good news for you in this book! God did leave Heaven for a little while. He came down to earth, people followed him about, and he showed them the will of God firsthand. HIS NAME WAS JESUS.

The Christ Conspiracy (Novel)   (retail) $10.00

What kind of child could potentially grow up to become a dangerous cult leader?

What would be the factors that propel his life toward inevitable destruction?

In *"The Christ Conspiracy,"* Jack Michael unfolds the uncanny rise and fall of a fictitious cult leader, and the decisions, ranging from the logical to the bizarre, that govern the ascent and descent.

Will God Supply All Your Needs?   (retail) $5.00

Philippians 4:19 is one of the most familiar, and one of the most claimed verses of scripture in the Bible!

"And my God shall supply all your need according to His riches in glory by Christ Jesus."

However, like other promises of God, there are some things we must FIRST do in order to qualify to receive the promise!

Foundation Building
(A Study Guide For Christians)   (retail) $12.00

(A spiral bound notebook containing 20 lessons designed to build a strong, biblical foundation in the lives of Christians, especially new Christians).

Jesus said: *"Therefore everyone who hears these words of mine and puts them into practice is like a wise man who built his house on the rock. The rain came down, the streams rose, and the winds blew and beat against that house; yet it did not fall, because it had its FOUNDATION on the rock."* (Matthew 7:24-25 NIV).

It is essential for every born-again Christian to have a strong, biblical foundation of God's word in their life. This is especially true during these tumultuous last days, because DECEPTION IS ABOUNDING, and will be ever increasing as we progress further into the End Times. When properly employed, this FOUNDATION BUILDING study course will help provide that strong foundation.

Whether you are the teacher or pupil, I challenge you as the Apostle Paul once challenged his spiritual son, Timothy: *"Be DILIGENT to present yourself approved to God, a worker who does not need to be ashamed, RIGHTLY DIVIDING* (rightly handling, accurately analyzing, skillfully teaching) *the word of truth."* (2 Timothy 2:15).

Grievous Wolves (Hindering spirits that Challenge and Oppose Spiritual Leadership)   (retail) $6.00

Satan fully intends to destroy the church of the Lord Jesus Christ. Now, perhaps you are thinking, *"Yes, those are his intentions, but he cannot do it, because the Bible says Jesus will build his church, and the gates of hell will not prevail against it."*

This is true. On the authority of the scriptures, Satan cannot destroy the church of Jesus Christ AS A WHOLE.

However, it is also an unfortunate truth that Satan and his agents have succeeded in destroying individual churches within the body of Christ.

One of the destructive forces that Satan has employed down through the ages is described by the Apostle Paul as GRIEVOUS WOLVES.

Why Haven't My Loved Ones Accepted Jesus Christ?   (retail) $6.00

"Very rarely will anyone die for a righteous man, though for a good man someone might possibly dare to die. But God demonstrates his own love for us in this: While we were still sinners, Christ died for us. Since we have now been justified by his blood, how much more shall we be saved from God's wrath through him!" (Romans 5:7-9 NIV).

With God's love and mercy leaping from the pages of the Bible through the above verses, and multiple other verses in the New Testament, one has to wonder why the world is not racing to accept Jesus Christ as their Lord and Savior?

How could anyone not desire forgiveness and cleansing of sin, and deliverance from the wrath of God? Why would anyone not desire to be clothed with the righteousness of God? How could anyone not desire to walk in harmony and fellowship with their creator?

It often seems like a great mystery, but actually, the Bible provides us with very clear answers as to why much of the world refuses to accept Jesus Christ.

Jack Michael Outreach Ministries
Ministry Newsletter

Most months, depending on outreach schedules and operational priorities, Jack Michael Outreach Ministries publishes a ministry newsletter.

Jack Michael is a FOUNDATION BUILDER. As such, you will quickly notice from the newsletters that he is committed to building a strong foundation of God's Word into the lives of God's people.

Jack Michael has been given the God-ordained assignment as a WATCHMAN ON THE WALLS in the body of Christ. As such, via the newsletter, he often deals with controversial issues that affect the body of Christ, and frequently warns God's people of existing or impending deception.

The ministry newsletter is brief, straightforward, and easily readable. It is available, free of charge, to God's people living in the United States, and also foreign countries.

For those who desire to receive the newsletter, PLEASE REQUEST IT. Send your clearly printed name/address to Jack Michael Outreach Ministries.

You may use the coupon on the following page, or send your request by facsimile.

To order books, or request the ministry newsletter, clip or copy the below order blank, enclose payment for books, and send to:

Jack Michael Outreach Ministries
P. O. Box 10688
Winston-Salem, NC 27108-0688

No postage is required for retail, domestic orders within the United States.

For wholesale orders, please contact Jack Michael Outreach Ministries at the above address, or:

Facsimile (336) 771-9698

Quantity	Title	Price
_____	_____	_____
_____	_____	_____
_____	_____	_____
_____	_____	_____

TOTAL ENCLOSED $_____

NAME _____

ADDRESS _____

_____